JUNK!

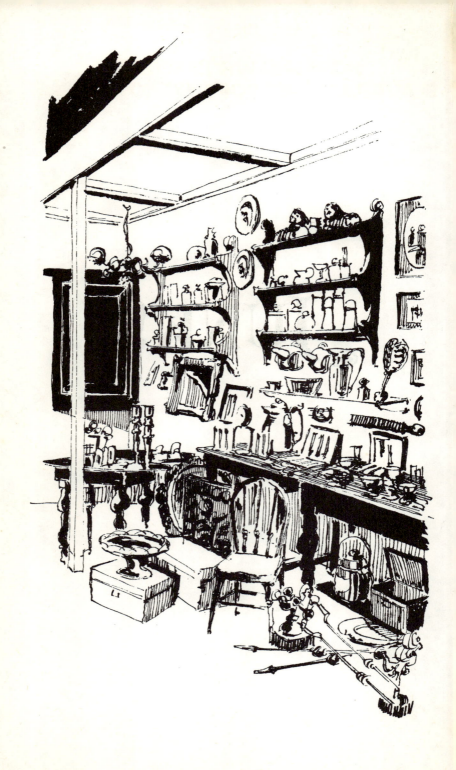

HOW AND WHERE TO BUY
BEAUTIFUL THINGS FOR NEXT TO NOTHING

JUNK!

DAVID
BENEDICTUS

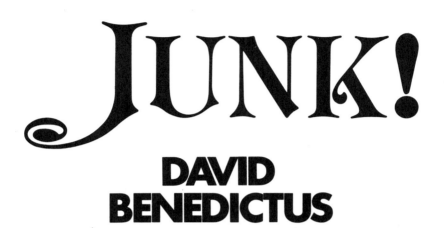

M

Drawings by Chris Partridge

ISBN 333 26941 1

First published 1976 by Macmillan London Ltd
London and Basingstoke
Associated companies in Delhi, Dublin,
Hong Kong, Johannesburg, Lagos, Melbourne,
New York, Singapore and Tokyo

Paperback edition published 1979

Filmset in 'Monophoto' Times 10 on 12 pt by
Richard Clay (The Chaucer Press), Ltd, Bungay, Suffolk
and printed in Great Britain by
Fletcher & Son Ltd, Norwich

British Library Cataloguing in Publication Data
Benedictus, David
  Junk!
  Index.
  ISBN 0–333–26941–1
  1. Title
  745.1   NK 1125
  Art objects—Collectors and collecting

Contents

Introduction

If there were a hundred dealers alone on a desert island, they would all make a profit.

Anon.

If a cynic is a man who knows the price of everything and the value of nothing, then the antique business is cynical beyond redemption. To the antique dealer everything has its price; he would sell his soul to the devil if he felt there was a sufficient profit margin on the deal. But ask him about values and he will go a little pale and slip a little pink pill into his mouth and change the subject to this incredible bargain he picked up at this church bazaar—the coffee spoons were not just silver but *Georgian* silver, and he bought them for fifty pence and the woman said she was afraid they were a bit grubby . . .

As to the public, by which in this context I mean those people who buy things to keep or to give as presents and not for resale, they know little about prices (but more than they used to, thanks to the many radio and television programmes, and books, such as this one, on the subject) but know how much they can afford; which, I suppose, is as good a definition of 'value' as any other. If the public knew more about prices, the profit margins of the dealers would shrink, until many of them went out of business. This would be an excellent thing, dealers being as necessary to the healthy evolution of our society as estate agents or solicitors or party political conferences—which is to say not necessary at all. I should know. I am a dealer myself.

In a small way. I run a weekly (and peripatetic) stall on which I sell things I buy from auctions, from jumble sales and from other dealers. And, if I have learned anything from the experience, it is that

      (a) It's amazing what people will buy,

and (b) It's amazing what people won't buy,

and (c) It's amazing how expensive things are in shops,

and (d) It's amazing how cheap things are on my stall,

and (e) It's amazing, despite (c) and (d) above, that so many people still go to shops, compared to the lucky few who buy from my stall.

Now this book is not intended for the specialist. There are admirable books crammed with information about coins, or Doulton china-marks, or Victorian jewellery, or snuff-boxes, and I hope to direct your attention to the most admirable book on each subject. But it is intended for the amateur collector, for those who have a crowded attic to empty or an empty house to fill; for those who don't know much about art but know what they like; and for those who are scared at the predators who hover around shop and stall and auction ready to swoop down and pick clean the bones of the unwary. It is for those who now the value of everything and the price of nothing, and it is for those who would like to earn, as I have done, a little bit on the side.

In the first part of the book you will find a guide to the mysterious rituals called auctions, with details of where to find one to suit your needs. You will be given the low-down on antique and collectors' fairs, the gen on charity shops, and a helping hand through the jungle of jumble sales.

In the second part I shall deal in greater detail with the different areas in which modest collectors operate, give hints as to what you should avoid and what embrace, and give some indication of the sort of prices you must be prepared to pay.

By the time you have reached the end of the book you will be a fully-fledged bargain-hunter, able to hold your own with all the other fully-fledged bargain-hunters who have read the book, a scourge to cheapskates and profiteers, a serendipitist.

There is only one rule for bargain-hunters, and it is this: Trust Your Own Judgment. Those things which most appreciate in value are the ones which over the years most people have found interesting or attractive; there can be no other criteria. Nor is price the only consideration. A single tea-cup which replaces a chipped one in an otherwise perfect set is a bargain, regardless (almost) of the price. And something which you think exquisite and which you decide you cannot live without, is priceless, and therefore, by definition, a bargain.

It is certainly true that, had you invested a legacy in a cross-section of antiques five, ten or twenty years ago you would now be rich beyond the dreams of avarice and certainly a great deal richer than if you had invested a similar sum in stocks and shares. Should we therefore conclude that collecting old things is a secure hedge against inflation? May it not rather be a thorny thicket to catch the horns of the unwary? Almost certainly it is both.

But, if you trust your own judgement and it proves leaky, you will at least be able to spend your declining years surrounded by objects which you, at least, find agreeable. The failed city investor has only old share certificates to comfort his old age, and all you can do with them is—but I promised Macmillan that I would not be vulgar.

PART 1

How and where to buy

One: The Auction

Attend no auctions if thou hast no money.
The Talmud

There are well over two hundred and fifty auction houses in Great Britain currently holding regular auctions of treasures, *objets d'art* and junk. At an average of fifteen auctions per auction house per annum and four hundred lots per auction, that's a million and a half falls of the gavel every year. Consequently all that is required of you if you are to make your fortune bargain-hunting is to find the best value from those million and a half lots; it can be done. I paid £9 at Graves, Son and Pilcher in Hove (and, in passing, auctioneers have names as colourful and appropriate as funeral parlours; there is even a Button, Menhenitt and Mutton in Wadebridge) for a large quantity of mixed English and oriental china. It was almost the cheapest lot of the day, but inside the Doulton tea-pot was a roll of £1 notes, thirty-six in all. There is no stall or shopholder who has not his or her own story to tell of such and such a bargain picked up for such and such a song at auction. They tend to be less garrulous (like me) when it comes to those disastrous purchases, the cunning fake, the well-concealed repair, the broken mechanism.

The art of the auction lies in the viewing, and your first obligation is to buy a catalogue. All but the most run-of-the-mill auctions of household goods will have printed catalogues. These cost between five and thirty pence (more at the very posh London salesrooms) and usually contain, besides the conditions of sale (which nobody reads), a disclaimer in words such as these: 'The buyer is deemed to have examined each lot and satisfied himself as to the condition quality description thereof before bidding. The Auctioneers are not responsible for the correct description or for the genuineness or authenticity of or any fault or deficiency in any lot and give no warranty whatever whether express or implied.'

A big saleroom will normally have experts to catalogue the items, and will be at some pains to give a fair description of each lot; other, less sophisticated houses will often settle for 'an armchair', 'a quantity of dinnerware', 'a silver tray', and suchlike.

Occasionally items in the catalogue will be italicised or printed in heavy type. Self-evidently this suggests that the auctioneers feel the item to be of some significance; so should you. It is also common for a horizontal line to be drawn under a lot; the meaning of this is that all the lots between two horizontal lines emanate from the same source. Where the goods on offer are from the estate of a dead person (or 'deceased' in auctioneer's jargon, which has a poetry all its own) this may be significant.

Once upon a time it was common practice for the contents of a house to be sold on the premises, and the practice still continues. But more frequently the better items from the house will be removed to the saleroom, where, in company with the better items from other houses, they will be sold off at a rather grand sale. The remnants will be sold on the premises, which may have a sad, looted, after-the-battle kind of atmosphere. The reason for this procedure is the problem of security in a private house which is open to viewers, and the difficulties auctioneers encounter in obtaining trustworthy porters for 'contents' sales. Consequently, in a provincial saleroom these days you may well find that the goods on view are the effects of several 'deceased persons' in the neighbourhood 'removed for convenience'.

Back to the catalogue, and a word of warning. Don't believe everything you read in auction catalogues—they are scarcely more reliable than the newspapers.

Catalogues (and I speak now of general rather than specialised sales) normally begin with lesser items. You must expect to have to munch your way through 'a white-painted bathroom cupboard and ditto stool', 'two lightweight suitcases and one other', 'six feather pillows, a lamp standard, and a leather pouffe' before reaching the jam. The reasoning behind this is obvious. People are late. People take a while to settle down. Adrenalin does not flow too eagerly at ten in the mornng. You have a right to complain if, as vendor, your goods are lots 1–22; the auctioneer with justice will reply that somebody's have to be.

Paradoxically you will rarely find all the goodies grouped together. They should, like treats for children or birthdays within a

family, be spaced out, so that each one is something of an event, and its glamour rubs off on those around it. In some East Anglian auctions (and Easterners are fervent auction-goers: local news-papers in Essex and neighbouring counties carry not only detailed advertisements for auctions to come, but detailed reports on auctions just past) there is a 'showcase section' at the end of the proceedings when the goods from the showcases, usually the better of the smaller items, are sold off in a swift-fire fusillade—no occasion for the slow-witted.

You may well find that some of the goods in the auction are subject to VAT. This will be indicated in the catalogue by an asterisk or cipher of some kind against the lots concerned. You may also be puzzled to see 'a.f.', 's.f.', or, very occasionally, 'v.f.' against catalogued items. 'A.f.' stands for 'as found' but what 's.f.' and 'v.f.' stand for is more obscure and I have never discovered. Some say that 's.f.' is 'slightly faulty' and 'V.F.S.' 'very faulty'; be that as it may, beware of 'a.f.', 's.f.', and 'v.f.'! Then there is that ominous suffix '-style', as in 'Sheraton-style', 'Staffordshire-style' and so forth. What it indicates, of course, is that the item does *not* have the style of Sheraton or Staffordshire, but would like to have. Watch out! And always remember that if the goods are faulty or not genuine, whatever the catalogue says about them, you have only yourself to blame. Sotheby's tell me that they plan to include in their catalogued descriptions of items a notation indicating that the goods have been repaired. Repairers have become so expert that such advice would be very welcome.

Where picture sales are concerned there is an elaborate code at work. Most cataloguers include the full Christian name or names of the artist, plus his surname, when they are convinced that the paint-ing is indeed a work by that artist. When the surname is preceded by initials, the suggestion is that the work is of the period of the artist and may be wholly or in part his work. But when only the artist's surname is given, the cataloguer believes that the painting is merely 'school of . . .' or 'in the style of . . .'. (Why they can't spell it out is another matter.) Similarly, 'After Turner' means a copy of a Turner, 'bears signature' or 'traces of signature' implies doubt about the signature, and 'bears date' or 'inscribed' implies doubt about the date.

If you are becoming alarmed (so soon!) it is quite permitted to ask the auctioneer's advice, or the porters'. The porters may also tell you what they expect a particular lot to fetch, and that probably means that the reserve is fixed below that figure, or that they have been asked to bid up to that figure by purchasers who cannot be present. I shall give you more about porters, reserves and commissioned bids in due course.

Having bought your catalogue, you must view; and you should be prepared to put aside an hour or more to do so. It helps, of course, to know what you are after. The book-dealers—anxious little men with discoloured moustaches—will waste no time on the china; the furniture folk—elegant Jensen-drivers with flashy cufflinks and manicured women—will be interested in little else, and the bric-à-brac set will be noisy and argumentative and get in everyone's way. But assuming that all you are after are *bargains*, you will have to view the lot. I like to view with my wife, Yvonne. We have separate catalogues and we view separately, comparing notes subsequently. More often than not we have priced things at much the same figure; where narrow variations exist we take an average; where there are wide fluctuations we ask each other why.

There are bound to be some lots you hanker after fervently, others you are less passionate about. It is as well to indicate which lots matter the most to you. If things go cheaply you may not be able to afford to buy everything you have marked, and it's as well to remind yourself constantly of your priorities. And, if prices are high, there is nothing shameful in leaving without buying a thing.

With goods which we intend to sell on our stall, we aim at a 100% mark-up and view accordingly. Thus, if the description of the lot is as follows: 'Cut-glass biscuit-barrel, sardine-dish, three-bottle cruet, plated cream jug, mustard pot and two condiments', we would reason as follows: 'Could sell the biscuit-barrel for £4·50, the sardine-dish for £3·00, the cruet for £1·25, the cream jug for £3·00, the mustard pot for £1·00 and the condiments for £1 the pair; total £13·75; 100% mark-up means we should stop bidding at £7.'

Naturally such a lot might take a while to sell and, with so much glass around, there's always the risk of breakages, so I might in the event stop short of £7, while 'Victorian mahogany oval swing mirror', priced at £20, would probably sell at once, so that £14, with a lower mark-up, would be a reasonable price to pay.

I was recently at an auction with my elegant friend, Mrs Amos. I bought 13 lots for a total outlay of £100. She spent £65 on an oak tantalus. My lots were cheap and the mark-up was well above the magical 100%; her lot was not cheap. But, when next we met, she had sold her tantalus for a profit of £19, while I had yet to recover most of my £100.

On some items the profit margins will be smaller than on others. And on the true treasures one cannot expect (and would not need) to make anything like 100%. It is very rare, for instance, for silver and gold to fetch less than their melt-down value. Everyone knows what they are worth; they're quoted every day in the financial columns, so there can be no excuse for ignorance. Nonetheless, insignificant pieces of silver are frequently to be found in such lots as: 'A quantity of table cutlery', and gold has a habit of hiding shyly in 'Jewellery box and contents'—hence my love of job lots, and, if you are a true bargain-hunter, yours too.

Viewing of job lots is a demanding exercise, at times even demeaning. People look at you with something of the same pity, mingled with contempt, which they reserve for old men picking their way through litter bins. ᐸut you don't mind that, do you? They always laughed at James Stewart in the first two reels; you too will have your due reward when the credits roll. Others who view job lots before you will hide away anything exceptional in the hope that those who follow them will miss these treasures. You, of course, will do the same, and I know somebody not a million miles from this typewriter who stands in front of the lot he has his eye on in order to obstruct the view of those who may not have spotted it. All's fair in love and auctions.

Do not be discouraged if goods are locked away in cupboards or cabinets; the porters have the keys and will be happy (probably) to unlock them for you. The cabinets are locked because the items within are deemed valuable; take the hint and inspect them carefully.

A digression concerning auction porters. They are unique. They have a look. They are short with round faces and they follow the horses. What is more to the point they know everything, not just about horses. While most are attached to one firm, some are cowboys and may be seen at country house auctions all over the place. There's nothing pleasanter than recognizing a friendly porter's face in a hostile marquee. They know which lots are damaged, which lots are fake, which dealers have an interest in which items, what the reserves are, and which are too high, who stole the gold chain, and why the auctioneer brought down his hammer so swiftly on lot 257. Some of them conduct a little buying and selling on their own account; most of them are rich; and most of them improbably susceptible to feminine charm. They will bid for you, record prices for you, find boxes for you, advise you. They are the salt of the earth. Savour them. For if the salt hath lost his savour wherewith shall ye be salted? God help you if you get a reputation for parsimony. End of digression on porters.

As a general rule it pays to be cynical at auctions. Expect things to be damaged. Run your finger around the rim of glasses. Check the legs of chairs and the private parts of tables. Take nothing on trust. The true professional, when confronted by something which is unexpectedly nice, will whistle airily, sneer, disparage the quality of the goods on display, or—as mentioned above—replace the item where it is not readily visible. As in a supermarket the most profitable items are the most efficiently displayed, so too in an auction room at the start of viewing; this is not always so at the end of the day!

When you have viewed you may wish to place a bid with a porter; many dealers rarely bother to attend a sale themselves. If you do leave a bid, you are taking a slight risk. The porter may forget to bid on your behalf, or he may start the bidding at your maximum. He may even use the information that you are prepared to bid £20 for lot 76 to entice another interested party to leave a bid of £21. My brother, who buys stamps, tells me that at philatelic sales the practice is to tip the porter a percentage of *the difference between your maximum and the price obtained*, which is sly. At some auctions you may be asked to fill out a slip with details of advance bids or make an entry in a 'bids book'. You may well buy the lot in this way, but you are unlikely to buy it for very much below your best price. Again some auctioneers will accept bids by telephone, though usually they will require you to have viewed the items and to be known to them. But really there is no substitute for attending the auction in person if you possibly can. It's splendid entertainment and with a witty auctioneer the time may pass more swiftly (almost certainly will) than if you were to buy best stalls for a West End Comedy Hit.

At Harrods Auction I have seen two porters dressed in full highland regalia; at Surbiton two ladies in dark blue and light blue coats were transformed into Oxford and Cambridge and the auction conducted in the style of the boat race; in Malmesbury a choleric farmer found himself trapped under a huge carpet and let fly such a stream of invective as would have soured the milk of an entire herd.

So now you've completed your viewing, priced the lots in which

17

you've an interest, and all that remains is to turn up on the right day, and bid.

You will need: plenty of newspaper and boxes for the smaller items; a pen or pencil to record the prices; a cheque book and means of identification (almost all auctioneers will accept cheques for moderate amounts, but it's often as well to check with them in advance—or check the details in the appended auctionography); a thermos of hot coffee and some tongue sandwiches with plenty of mustard; and an undemanding book, or crossword puzzle. I find crossword puzzles ideal for auctions. They are not so absorbing that you miss your cues, and yet they keep your hands busy!

The first thing to be remembered as the auction gets under way is not to be carried away by the mass hysteria which sometimes affects otherwise level-headed folk. It seems to strike most particularly at country house auctions, where the elegance of the surroundings can induce a dangerous euphoria. (Although I should add that there are other valid reasons for the high-flying prices at country-house auctions. Dealers like buying 'first-time' goods; things which have self-evidently not been on the market before and are unlikely to be faked. It's something similar to the attraction that elderly Japanese gentlemen have for young virgins, so much so that special establishments—but now *I'm* getting carried away.) Mass lethargy can also affect auction crowds; and these moments, of course, are the moments when you need to be at your most alert.

There are usually seats available, and always if you arrive in good time. It's obviously helpful to sit close to the spot where the goods are displayed for you're bound to have missed something in the viewing, and also advisable to sit where the auctioneer can readily see you. Don't be alarmed about sneezing or scratching your head at inopportune moments. There is a popular myth, fostered by stand-up comics, that you can thus land yourself with some unwanted monstrosity. I've never known it to happen. And if a lot, which you decidedly did not want, is knocked down to you in error, most auctioneers will offer it for resale forthwith.

You may bid in a number of ways, some nod their heads, some wave their hands, some shout out; I usually bid with my catalogue, since it is easily observable. It's helpful to put your bids in early. If you save the auctioneer's time, he may be on your side, and wield his hammer to your advantage later on. But be warned; if the auctioneer attempts to start the bidding at £10 you should not necessarily leap in, even though you may be prepared to go to £15.

If you wait for him to lower his asking price, you might get it for £5.

Most auctioneers take bids in units of 50p or £1 to £10, of £1 up to £20, and either of £5 or at a progression of £2, £3, £3, £2 (viz. £22—£25—£28—£30), to £100. Above £100 expect the bidding to rise by £5 or £10, above £1000 by £25, £50 or £100. At small country auctions bids of less than 50p may be countenanced (I watched with pity and incredulity the entire contents of a Falmouth bedroom, including curtains, carpets, the lot, being sold for 20p), and it is always permitted—though unpopular—to offer a bid at an intermediate price.

Some auctioneers (Phillips at their Lisson Grove rooms for instance) only call out the lot number and the briefest description of each lot, and sometimes not even that, so that the action is fast and furious, and you had better be fast if you don't want to be furious. Other auctioneers insist on each item beng found and held up for admiration before bidding can begin. It's a general rule that most auctioneers aim at a hundred lots per hour, a rate which they never quite achieve.

And what about cabals, cadres and cartels? Hard-faced men in white ties and co-respondent shoes who fix the bidding in advance only to hold informal auctions themselves afterwards in the dingy back parlours of smoke-filled snooker-halls? It happens, of course. And most especially in those areas of the country where there are only a few serious dealers in rivalry. Unquestionably they do agree not to compete openly for certain items, and who is to blame them? In any case such dubious activities can only work to your advantage, unless you happen to be the vendor, in which case you are certainly unfortunate and usually deceased.

'What are we supposed to do about it', the man from Sotheby's plaintively inquired, 'if you and some friends of yours decide to get together?' I began to feel sorry for the poor chap. He looked as if he hadn't eaten for a week (smoked salmon, that is). But then he weakened his case by continuing: 'It's true that our staff can buy for themselves, but in full competition with everyone else.' I should have thought that, if jockeys are not permitted to bet, nor doctors reveal their case-histories, nor husbands give evidence against wives, nor journalists reveal their sources of information, it is equally improper for the employees of auction houses to put in bids. But there again perhaps I'm just an old fogey.

Almost all auctioneers maintain (but see the Auctionography) that their reserve prices are never revealed, but a very grand dealer of my acquaintance (the sort of man who is so grand that he doesn't even need to carry a cheque book) assured me that this was very far from being the case: 'Naturally,' he argued, 'you can't expect somebody to travel from Geneva or New York for a single item, if the reserve on that item has been set above what he is prepared to pay.' I remain unconvinced, but international art dealers are above and beyond the natural laws that rule the lives of the rest of us. Most of the poshest salerooms now include with their catalogues an 'estimated price', which goes some way towards resolving the problem of reserves, but the estimates tend to be both vague and unreliable.

It is perhaps just worth mentioning another dodge which on occasion I have seen employed, though usually to very little effect. And this is the dodge which one might classify as Talking Things Down. The way it works is this. Three dealers are competing for a fine Queen Anne bureau. They are fairly confident that there is no one at the auction with enough money to compete against them, but just to be on the safe side, when the lot is called Dealer A will announce in a stage whisper: 'It's riddled with worm' and Dealer B will add: 'One of the feet is half off' and Dealer C will chip in with: 'Have you *seen* the handles!' Of course to the thinking man such unanimity of opinion on the demerits of what seems to him to be an attractive piece (added to the fact that Dealer A can thereafter be seen to be reluctantly bidding for the piece he so roundly disparaged) must make the bureau *more* attractive not less, but the thinking man's protection against such tomfoolery—yours too—is to view carefully, decide what the thing is worth to you, and bid up to that price, and not beyond. No ghoulies, ghosties, nor long-leggity beasties can hurt you then. And it will not be you who goes bump in the night.

It is still possible to purchase outstanding bargains at auction, and will be so long as there are men and women in the country with more money than patience and less discernment than you. It is also possible, probable even, that you will at times pay through the nose for trash (on one black-letter day I paid £5 for two broken, fake horn gramophones, made under licence in Spain, one without a needle, one without a horn). But if you find an auction where the prices seem generally low, buy there. And, if you find an auction where the prices seem generally high, sell there.

Selling at an auction is an altogether more speculative business than buying at one, for this reason: that so much of the process is out of your control. You have little say in how your goods are to be catalogued, or where they are to be displayed, or when they are to be sold. You can of course insist on fixing a reserve (see above), but you risk losing the 'buying-in' fee, which usually runs at from $2\frac{1}{2}\%$ to 5% of the reserve—although some auctioneers will waive this fee if they have been consulted as to the reserve. An alternative, which most auctioneers permit, is that, in place of a reserve, you should be present and bid on your own behalf, or have a friend to do it for you. In this case you may boldly succeed in bumping the price up beyond the reserve you might have fixed, but risk, of course, paying the full commission should the final bid be your bid. I have known an auctioneer to put in 'false bids' of his own when he felt that a lot was not reaching what it deserved to reach, and I was somewhat alarmed when some items which I had put into his auction and which I had heard people bid for, were returned to me as unsold. The auctioneer blandly confessed that he had made some bids on my behalf, and thought that I should have been grateful.

But you can do something to ensure that you receive a fair price for your possessions. You can present them to the auctioneer in as attractive a light as possible, although this does not necessarily mean that everything should be clean and spruce. An old picture, for instance, is likely to fetch a better price if the frame is cobwebby and the canvas a little torn, than if it is restored, revarnished, reframed and glazed.

It is important to inquire of the auctioneer, before putting your lots into his auction, how long it is likely to be before they are sold. Normally you would expect your goods to be put into the next available sale, and you would receive your cheque some fortnight after the auction, but it may be in your interest to accept the auctioneer's advice and wait for the next specialist sale. A doll's house, for instance, may well fetch more if sold in a specialist toy sale than in a general sale of furniture and effects. And since an auctioneer has an interest in obtaining the best possible price for your goods, you disregard his advice at your peril.

Paradoxically it is not always at the smart London houses that the best prices are obtainable, and some London dealers make it a regular practice to put one or two good items in a number of provincial sales, where the interest aroused by exceptional quality may lead to more competitive bidding than in the jaded metropolis where nothing is new under the smog.

Finally it's worth pointing out that there is no good reason why you should not choose to run an auction yourself. Should you be the executor or beneficiary of this large and beautifully furnished estate (or tiny and tatty) you can save a lot of money by *not* employing a firm of estate agents and auctioneers. (How much you will save is likely to be 15% of the proceeds less the costs of porterage, publicity, security and so on, or about $7\frac{1}{2}\%$ net.) All you will need to do is to display the items clearly ticketed with the lot numbers, produce catalogues which need not describe the goods in any great detail, circulate posters and throwaways in the neighbourhood, and advertise in the local press. If you fancy the idea of conducting the bidding yourself, you will need an assistant to record the bids, and possibly a 'heavy' to direct attention to each lot; but it might be less risky to hire an auctioneer to take charge of this side of things. You could even go halves with anyone else similarly placed.

You will probably be amazed at the interest shown in such a venture. The merest hint of amateurism will bring the bargain-hunters out in droves, and, should you also hire a caterer and provide alcoholic beverages, there's no knowing how much money you may make. In any case it could be a lot of fun.

And if, after reading the above, you are fired with enthusiasm to attend an auction, but don't know where to find one, then I suggest reference to:

a) The property section of your local paper.

b) The Yellow Pages.

c) Publications such as *Art and Antiques Weekly*, which contains a reasonably complete list of forthcoming sales.

d) The *Daily Telegraph* on a Monday, *The Times* on a Tuesday, or the *Guardian* (for auctions in the Manchester area) on a Saturday.

or best of all

e) My carefully compiled Auctionography below.

Auctionography

This selective list of auctions and salerooms is divided by area, and within each area the names are given in alphabetical order. The information was culled from answers to a questionnaire, and the questions (to which the numbered answers correspond) are as follows:

1. Name of firm
2. Address or addresses
3. How often do they hold auctions (excluding property)
   a) On their own premises?
   b) On private premises?
4. In what area or areas of the country do they chiefly operate?
5. Are their auctions
   a) General?
   b) Specialist?
6. What rates of commission do they charge
   a) To vendor?
   b) To purchaser?
7. Do they accept reserves, and if so, on what terms?
8. Are their reserve prices made known either before or during the sale?
9. Do they accept bids from the vendor?
10. Do they accept bids in advance?
11. Do they accept bids by telephone?
12. On what day of the week/month do they hold their auctions?
13. When is their viewing?
14. Have they noticed any significant trend or trends in the prices paid at their auctions in the last two years?
15. Do they provide
    a) Catalogues?
    b) Transportation?
16. Do they take cheques, and, if so, under what circumstances?
17. What limitations do they impose—if any—on accepting goods for auction?
18. Is there a waiting time? If so, how long before goods are put up for sale?
19. Are the majority of their lots in the range
    a) up to £5
    b) £5–£10
    c) £50–£25
    d) £25–£50
    e) £50–£100
    f) £100–£1000
    g) above £1000
20. Any other information?

South Coast Area (Kent, Sussex, Hampshire and Isle of Wight)

Baker Donnelly (inc. Michael G. Baker) 2. 4 Latimer Street, **Romsey**, Hants 3a. 2–3 times per month 3b. 1–2 times per annum 4. Hampshire area 5a. General—monthly sales, Specialist—quarterly 5b. Coins and Medals; Books, stamps, documents, etc.; silver, plate and jewellery, etc.; each five per annum 6a. Silver 12½%; all other 15%, except important items at 10% 6b. Nil 7. Yes, no sale, no charge 8. No 9. Yes 10. Yes 11. Yes 12. Sats (general) 13. Day prior and morning of sale 14. Silver up 20%–60%; paintings down 15%–30% 15a. Yes 15b. No 16. Yes, if known, otherwise with bankers' card 17. Virtually none 18. Usually 4–6 weeks 19. — 20. Goods graded so that good quality and general goods are not mixed in the same auction.

Burrows 2. 39/41 Bank Street, **Ashford**, Kent 3a. Monthly 3b. 6 per annum 4. Kent 5a. General 5b. — 6a. 15% on single lots, 12½% on lots of £50+ 6b. None 7. Yes, as agreed with vendor 8. No 9. Only if no reserve fixed 10. Yes 11. Yes, if confirmed in writing 12. Variable 13. Day prior 14. Impossible to detail 15a. Yes 15b. Yes 16. Yes, if known or references supplied 17. No trade goods 18. About 4 weeks 19. £25–£50 20. 'Endeavour to produce an honest catalogue and do not over-describe.'

Butler and Hatch Waterman 2. Mrs Pauline Chalk, 102 High Street, **Tenterden**, Kent 3a. Monthly at Tenterden, bi-monthly at Hythe 3b. 3–4 per annum 4. South of Maidstone, 25-mile radius 5a. General 5b.— 6a. 15% 6b. None 7. Yes, no charge 8. No 9. Yes occasionally, especially at private house sales. No charge 10. Yes 11. Yes if regulars 12. Thursdays (Tenterden, 4-weekly), Wednesdays (Hythe, 8-weekly) 13. Tenterden: Sunday and Tuesday prior; Hythe: Tuesday prior 14. High prices maintained for really good pieces 15a. Yes 15b. No 16. Yes, with reference or card 17. Only good quality 18. No 19. £25–£50 20. Increasing number of sales.

Churchman's Auction Gallery (*Churchman, Burt & Son*) 2. High Street, **Steyning**, Sussex BN4 3LA; also **Horsham, Worthing and Billingshurst** 3a. Twice monthly 3b. As requested 4. Sussex 5a. General & Specialist 5b. Silver stamps & coins etc. 6a. 15% private; 10% trade 6b. Not if reserve agreed with us 7. No 8. No 9. Only if no reserve 10. Yes 11. Yes 12. Thursdays and Saturdays (first in each month) 13. Day prior 14. Follow cost of living, but pictures, particularly 19th Century, lag behind 15a. Yes 15b. Yes 16. By prior arrangement 17. Saleability 18. Maximum 1 month. Payment 3 days after sale 19. £10–£1,000 20. —.

Grave, Son & Pilcher 2. 71 Church Road, **Hove** BN3 2GL and 51 Old Steine, **Brighton** BN1 1HU 3a. Average monthly 3b. As instructed 4. Brighton Hove and environs 5a. General and Specialist 5b. Various 6a. Scaled up to 15% 6b. None 7. Yes, by agreement with us 9. No 10. Discouraged 11. Yes 12. Mondays and Tuesdays 13. Private Thursdays; general public Friday and Saturday 14. Erratic but rising 15a. Yes 15b. No, but liaise with local carman 16. Yes, if (a) known, (b) small amount, or (c) by checking with bank 17. Good standard. Trade goods only rarely   18. 3–4 weeks, max.   19. £25–£100   20. —.

Heathfield Furniture Auctions   2 The Market, **Heathfield**, Sussex (tel: Heathfield 2132)   3a. Weekly (General), Monthly (Antique and Victoriana)   3b. Rarely   4. East Sussex   5a. General   5b.–6a. 15%   6b. None   7. Yes   8. No   9. Yes, if no reserve   10. Yes   11. Known clients   12. Tuesdays weekly, Thursdays monthly   13. Day prior   14. Increase in trade for 'shipping furniture'   15a. Yes   15b. Yes   16. Known clients   17. None   18. 3–4 weeks   19. £0–£10 weekly, £10–£100 monthly   20. Weekly sale, mainly household furniture, delivered and sold on day of sale.

Hobbs, Parker   2. 9 Tufton Street, **Ashford**, Kent (also at **Maidstone**)   3a. Several times weekly   3b. Twenty-five times a year   4. Kent, East Sussex   5a. Both   5b. Various   6a. Varies, usually 10%   6b. None   7. Yes, no terms   8. No   9. Yes, reluctantly   10. Yes   11. Yes   12. Every day except Sunday   13. Day of sale   14. Firm prices for all goods   15a. Yes   15b. Can be arranged   16. Yes, with reference or card   17. None   18. None   19. —   20. —.

John Hogbin and Son   2. 15 Cattle Market, **Sandwich** and 53 High Street, **Tenterden**, Kent (tel: Sandwich 3641/2/3, Tenterden 2241)   3a. No   3b. Yes   4. Sandwich and Tenterden   5a. General   5b. —   6a. 15%   6b. None   7. Yes   8. No   9. No   10. Yes   11. Yes, subject to written confirmation   12. Wednesday   13. Day prior   14. —   15a. Yes   15b. No   16. Yes, subject to verification   17. No bedsteads or wardrobes   18. No   19. Up to £100   20. —.

King and Chasemore   2. Pulborough Sale Rooms, Station Road, **Pulborough**, Sussex   3a. Fortnightly   3b. Every two months   4. Every part of Britain, also Europe, N. America, Australia   5a. Specialist   5b. Furniture, painting, silver, glass, books, clocks, etc.   6a. 15%   6b. None   7. Yes, by agreement   8. No, but estimates are available   9. Yes   10. Yes   11. Yes   12. Every other Tuesday/Wednesday and Thursday   13. Saturday and Monday before the sales   14. Generally upward   15a. Yes—illustrated   15b. Firm of carriers affiliated to art department   16. Yes, but bank references if unknown   17. No limitations   18. 3–4 weeks   19. £50–£1,000   20. Turnover in excess of £1m per annum.

Parsons, Welch and Cowell   2. 129 High Street, **Sevenoaks**, Kent   3a. Monthly   3b. On hired premises   4. Home counties   5a. General auctions in specialist items   5b. —   6a. 15%   6b. Nil   7. Yes   8. No   9. No   10. Yes   11. Yes   12. Wednesdays and Thursdays   13. Day prior to first day of sale   14. Generally upward, less so for more recent and poorer quality items   15a. Yes   15b. Yes   16. Usually, but bankers' card above £20, and check with bank for larger amounts   17. Not household appliances, bed linens etc. Prefer good quality   18. Up to one month   19. Any prices   20. —.

Sir Francis Pittis & Son   2. Cross Street Saleroom, **Newport**, Isle of Wight and Chapel Street Saleroom, **Newport**, Isle of Wight (tel: Newport 2011)   3a. Fortnightly   3b. 6 times per annum   4. Isle of Wight   5a. Mainly general   5b. —   6a. 15% General, 12½% Specialist   6b. Yes. 5% no-sale commission   8. No   9. Yes   10. Yes, on condition purchaser has viewed 11. Yes, ditto 12. Usually Thursday 13. General sales, morning of sale; specialist sales, day prior 14. Good modern furniture up by 50% 15. Silver, small antiques, jewellery, paintings up by 25%–30% 15a. Yes 15b. Arrangements made at owners risk 16. Yes, subject to bankers' reference 17. Saleability 18. General, one month; antiques, two months 19. £10–£25 20. —.

Riddetts of Bournemouth (formerly Riddett and Adams Smith) 2. The Auction Galleries, Richmond Hill, **Bournemouth** 3a. Fortnightly (1,800 lots) 3b. Only if worth it 4. Whole of Wessex 5a. Both—General above average goods, also Specialist 5b. Various 6a. 15% + 15p per lot + VAT 6b. Nil 7. Yes, 5% on reserve price but less if reserve fixed by us, and not reached 8. No 9. Yes, but discouraged 10. Yes, but don't sell in advance of auctions 11. Not unless bidder known to be reliable 12. Every other Tues., Wed., Thurs. (and sometimes Friday) 13. Monday prior, also Saturday prior to special customers 14. Prices peaked in '73/4, decrease of about 10% since, but no downward trend in fine pieces 15a. Yes 15b. No, but can introduce buyer to carrier 16. Only from regulars. Otherwise check bank, and hold goods (if customer demurs) until cheque is cleared 17. Must be clean and saleable 18. Goods sold within week of receipt, but specially fine items held back for specialist sales. Accounts paid after 3 weeks 19. £10–£25 General, £100–£1,000 Specialist 20. —.

James B. Terson & Sons 2. 27/29 Castle Street, **Dover** 3a. Every 2 weeks 3b. Never 4. East Kent 5a. General 5b. — 6a. 15% 6b. None 7. Yes, 10% buying-in fee, unless reserve suggested by us 8. No 9. No 10. Yes, if known 11. Yes, if known 12. Fridays 13. Afternoon before and day of sale 14. Quality more important than age 15a. Yes 15b. Yes 16. Yes, bankers' card or known customers 17. Must be saleable 18. 2 weeks 19. £10–£25 20. Virtually anything sold.

Way, Riddett 2. Town Hall Chambers, Lind Street, **Ryde**, Isle of Wight 3a. Monthly 3b. 4 per annum 4. Isle of Wight 5a. Yes 5b. Specialist every two months 6. 15% + VAT on commission 6b. Nil 7. Yes, 5%. No sale, no commission 8. No 9. Yes 10. Yes 11. Yes, on condition they know address and 'phone number 12. Thursday, specialists, and occasionally Wednesday 13. Day prior 14. General trend upwards, especially Victorian and Edwardian furniture for export. Silver, pictures and plate also up, but more slowly 15a. Yes, free to trade 15b. Own carrier and transportation to mainland by local firms 16. Yes, if known, otherwise by identification 17. Reasonable standard of cleanliness 18. General sales a month, specialist longer 19. £10–£25 20. —.

Worsfolds 2. 40 Station Road, **West Canterbury**, Kent 3a. Monthly 3b. 2/3 per annum 4. East Kent 5a. Usually general, occasionally specialist 5b. Bronzes, pictures, silver 6a. 15% 6b. None 7. Not below £15; 5% or 2½% if fixed by us 8. No 9. No, in saleroom 10. Yes 11. Yes 12. Thursdays 13. Wednesdays 14. — 15a. Yes 15b. Arrangement with local carrier 16. Only if known to them 17. No rubbish 18. No 19. Approx. £20 20. —.

East Anglia (including Lincolnshire)

A. E. Spear & Sons 2. **Wickham Market**, Suffolk 3a. Weekly 3b. Sometimes 4. 20 miles' radius 5a. General 5b. – 6a. 10% 6b. None 7. Yes, unconditional 8. No 9. Yes 10. Yes 11. Yes 12. Mondays 13. Saturday prior 14. General rise across the board; 50% increase in shipping goods 15a. Yes, once a month 15b. Yes, by arrangement 16. Yes 17. Saleability; antique bias 18. 2–4 weeks 19. £5–£300 20. 1,500 lots per month.

Chas. Boardman & Son 2. Station Road Corner, **Haverhill**, Suffolk 3a. Monthly 3b. Mainly at Town Hall, Clare 4. East Anglia 5a & b. General and Specialist: oak and period decor, paintings, porcelain 6a. 15% up to £500, 10% over £500, over £1,500 by arrangement; minimum £1 per lot 6b. Nil 7. Yes, no fee if agreed reserve, otherwise normal commission 8. Always confidential 9. No 10. Yes 11. Only if already viewed 12. Usually Wednesdays, occasionally Tuesdays or Thursdays 13. 2–7 p.m. on day previous and morning of sale 14. Specialist oak sales (held every 3 months) attract large number of continental buyers with accompanying upward trend; prices of general sales steady 15a. Yes 15b. Arranged 16. Yes, by arrangement or bankers' ref. 17. All items inspected before acceptance 18. Next suitable sale 19. £100–£1,000 20. Widely advertised

William H. Brown & Son 2. 33 Watergate, **Grantham**, Worthgate House, **Sleaford** and 21 offices 3a. 6 per annum 3b. 6 per annum 4. East, esp. Lincs 5a. & b. General and Specialist (guns, books, coins, etc) 6a. 12% 6b. 5% 7. Yes, no terms 8. No 9. No 10. Yes 11. Yes 12. Wednesdays and Thursdays 13. Previous day 14. Very good prices for clean, good quality antiques; items show an upward trend of 20–30%, paintings and pictures depressed over the last two years. Prices slightly down on 1973 levels, but now signs of increase 15a. Yes 15b. Yes, arranged but not provided 16. Yes, known clients or bankers' reference 17. None 18. 2 months between sales 19. £10–£25 20. Also regular car and agricultural machinery sales and country house sales, irregularly.

Cooper Hirst F.R.I.C.S. 2. Goldway House, Parkway, **Chelmsford** CM2 7PR 3a. Every Friday at Chelmsford Market 3b. Infrequently 4. Chelmsford and mid-Essex 5a. & b. General 6a. 12½% 6b. Nil 7. Yes 8. No 9. Only in special circumstances 10. Only from known purchasers 11. Only from known purchasers 12. Every Friday 13. Day of sale 14. Steady increase 15a. Not for weekly, only for special sales 15b. Can be arranged 16. Yes, with bankers' reference 17. None 18. No 19. Up to £100 20. Furniture, bric-à-brac, builders' materials, farm implements, poultry, rabbits, produce, etc. Private sales can be arranged in hired halls or on premises.

Fennwright, Garrod, Turner 2. 50 St Nicholas St, **Ipswich** 3a. Approximately monthly 3b. Approx. 5 per annum 4. Local 5. In 4 sections: (a) silver, (b) pictures and books, (c) porcelain, bronzes, etc., (d) furniture and clocks; spread over two days 6a. 15%, 10% over £400 7. Yes, no sale, no charge 8. No 9. Only if there are no reserves 10. Yes 11.

27

Yes 12. Thursdays, Fridays 13. Wednesday previous 14. Far too many changes to comment briefly 15a. Yes 15b. Can arrange 16. If known 17. Must be up to standard 18. Up to six weeks 19. £10–£100, some up to £5000 20. Going since 1770; Noel Turner chairman of R.I.C.S. Furniture and Works of Art Committee.

Flick & Son 2. Old Bank House, **Saxmundham** and 139 High Street **Aldeburgh** 3a. Monthly 3b. Once or twice per annum 4. East Suffolk 5a. & b. General mainly 6a. $5\frac{1}{2}\%$ 6b. Nil 7. Yes, normal buying-in fee 8. No 9. No 10. Only if bid is in form of a commission to purchase and the bidder has seen or knows the article 11. Yes, but need confirmation in writing except where well known to us 12. Friday, except private house sales 13. Day before 14. Upward trend for three years for majority of categories, and recently hand-made furniture 15a. Yes 15b. No 16. Yes, previously unknown customers arrange in advance 17. Must be up to standard 18. Month following 19. £5–£100 except in specialist sales 20. Valuations also given.

James—Norwich Auctions 2. 33 Timber Hill, **Norwich** 3a. No 3b. Once a month at the Maid's Head Hotel 4. Norfolk, but mostly overseas 5a. & b. General and Specialist (stamps, coins, etc) 6a. 10–15% 6b. Nil 7. Yes, providing reasonable, 5% charge if goods unsold 8. No 9. No 10. Yes 11. Yes, from known clients 12. Saturdays 12–5 13. Saturday mornings at hotel, previous day at office 14. Stamps continually rising (especially British) 15a. Yes, £4 p.a. in UK 15b. Yes, charged to buyer 16. Yes, with references 17. Good quality, not less than £3 18. 6–10 weeks 19. £10–£25 20. 75% of lots sold to postal bidders, two-thirds of whom are foreigners.

G. A. Key 2. 3 Market Place, Aylsham, **Norwich** 3a. Weekly (general); monthly (antique); bi-monthly (pictures) 3b. From time to time 4. East Anglia, chiefly N. Norfolk 5. General and specialist (oils, watercolours and prints) 6a. $12\frac{1}{2}\%$; 10% on bills not paid within week of purchase 7. Yes 8. No 9. Yes, but discourage 10. Yes 11. Yes, if client is known 12. General Mondays, monthly Tuesdays, bi-monthly Fridays 13. General Sat 9–10.30 a.m.; monthly, morning of sale and day prior 2.30 p.m.–8.30 p.m. 14. Inferior pictures 30% downward trend; better class pictures steady; antiques and silver similar; better quality shipping items steady to upward 15a. Yes 15b. Yes 16. Yes, with regulars, otherwise check with bank 17. No 18. No, next available sale 19. General, a–b; antique pictures, a–f.

Lacy, Scott & Sons 2. 3 Hatter St, **Bury St Edmunds**, Suffolk 3a. 8 per annum 3b. Occasionally 4. East Anglia 5a. & b. General, and Specialist occasionally—silver and paintings 6a. $12\frac{1}{2}\%$ 6b. Nil 7. Yes, $2\frac{1}{2}\%$ if unsold 8. Never 9. Only in absence of reserve 10. Yes, on items previously viewed 11. Yes, ditto, but only from those well known to auctioneers 12. Tuesdays/Saturdays 13. Day prior to and morning of sale 14. Overall downward trend in all areas, lately halted 15a. Yes 15b. Averaged and charged 16. Yes 17. At our discretion 18. 2 months 19. £25–£30.

Neal & Tuomy 2. 18 High Street, **Aldeburgh** 3a. Held at Jubilee Hall, Aldeburgh 3b. Occasionally 4. Aldeburgh and district 5a. & b. General only   6a. 15% to £50, 12½% thereafter   6b. Nil   7. Yes, must be arranged and commission as if sold   8. During sale   9. Yes, in certain cases   10. Yes, in writing   11. Yes, but reluctantly, from those known to us   12. Thursdays   13. Wednesday prior to sale   14. Victoriana sells well   15a. Yes   15b. Yes   16. Yes, if known to us   17. No old beds, mattresses, cookers unless very clean   18. Up to 6 weeks   19. All prices.

Norman Wright & Hodgkinson   2. 40 High Street, **Stamford**   3a. Monthly   3b. As occasion demands   4. North Cambridgeshire and South Lincolnshire   5a. & b. Usually General and some Specialist (Period Furniture and Victoriana)   6a. 10%–15%   6b. Nil   7. Yes   8. Never   9. Never   10. Yes   11. Not as a rule   12. Wednesdays or Saturdays   13. Day before   14. Furniture has done extremely well   15a. Yes   15b. No, but arranged   16. From known buyers   17. None, providing saleable   18. No   19. £10–£25   20. Also live and dead stock, trade stock, etc.

G. E. Sworder & Sons   2. 19 North St., **Bishops Stortford**   3a. Fortnightly   3b. Very occasionally   4. Herts. and Sussex   5a. & b. General and specialist   6a. Modern 15%; Antique 12½%   6b. Nil   7. Yes, no sale, nominal charge   8. No   9. Yes   10. Yes, in writing   11. Only from known persons   12. Tuesdays   13. Sat a.m. and Monday   14. Nil   15a. Yes   15b. Yes   16. Yes, with references   17. Quality, saleability   18. Usually 1 month, sometimes quicker   19. All prices   20. Old established firm, house clearance work of all types.

Edwin Watson & Son   2. 22 North Street, **Bishops Stortford**   3a. 5 general furniture per annum; 8 pictures, silver and jewellery per annum   3b. Periodically   4. East Anglia   5a. & b. General & Specialist   6a. 12½% on specialist, 15% on general   6b. Nil   7. Yes   8. No   9. No   10. Yes   11. Yes   12. Bishops Stortford, Thursdays; Colchester, Saturdays; Saffron Walden, Tuesdays   13. Day prior to and evening of sale   14. Good lots still greatly in demand, restored and modern down by 25%–30%   15a. Yes   15b. Yes   16. Yes, after references   17. None   18. 14–28 days   19. Junk £5–£10, specialist £25–£30 up to £1,000   20. Total turnover 80–100,000 lots per annum.

J. M. Welch & Son   2. The Old Town Hall, **Dunmow**, Essex   3a. 5–6 per annum   3b. Seldom   4. Essex   5a. & b. General, 2 or 3 times per annum; specialist (antiques) 5 or 6 per annum   6a. 15%   6b. Nil   7. Yes (no commission if reserve fair)   8. No   9. Yes, but discouraged   10. Yes   11. Yes   12. Mondays   13. Fri/Sat prior to sale   14. Greatly up due to buyers from overseas   15a. Yes   15b. Arranged   16. Yes   17. No trade entries   18. 3–4 months   19. £10–£50, but up to excess of £200   20. Try to take only genuine items from private houses and disposal of entire households.

West Country and Wales

Bruton Knowles & Co   2. Albion Chambers, 55 Barton Street, **Gloucester**   3a. None   3b. 30 per annum   4. Mainly Gloucestershire and surrounding counties   5. Both   6a. 7½% plus advertising, printing, portering, etc.   6b. None   7. Yes, no charge if lot not sold   8. No   9. No   10. Yes   11. Yes, if known   12. Any day   13. Usually day prior   14. All prices have been rising   15a. Yes   15b. No   16. Yes   17. Must be from private houses   18. About six weeks   19. All prices   20. Valuations and sales under direction of Arthur Negus, who has been with the firm 28 years.

Button, Menhenitt and Mutton   2. Belmont Auction Rooms, **Wadebridge**, Cornwall; also at **Bodmin** and **Padstow**   3a. Alternate months (4 days) antiques, etc. and general household, etc.   3b. Some valuables removed to salerooms   4. Cornwall and Devon   5a. & b. General and Specialist (coins, medals, stamps)   6a. 10–12½%   6b. 5%   7. Yes, 5% on unsold lots, imposed at their discretion   8. No, but estimates are given and if price approaches reserve it is declared; sometimes offers made SVC (Subject to Vendor's Consent)   9. Yes, if no reserve   10. Yes   11. Yes   12. Tuesday–Friday (4-day auctions): Tuesdays—coins and medals; Wednesdays—household; Wednesdays—stamps   13. Monday and throughout the 4-day auctions; coins and stamps on day, since they are evening sales   14. No significant trends, except greater competition for more important unrestored items   15a. Yes   15b. Yes   16. Yes, if prior arrangement or bankers' card   17. None   18. No   19. £5–£1,000+   20. Cater for all buyers and sellers, will accept a single minor piece from an OAP to big consignments from executors, trade and collectors. No minimum charge and consider they offer a service to all sections of the public.

Cambray Auction Galleries (*Cavendish House of Cheltenham*)   2. 26 Cambray Place, **Cheltenham**, GL50 2LX   3a. Monthly (excl. August)   3b. Occasionally, if necessary   4. 50 miles of Cheltenham   5. General   6a. 15%   6b. None   7. Yes, subject to agreement   8. No   9. No   10. Yes   11. Yes, if confirmed in writing   12. Mondays to Wednesdays   13. Previous Friday, trade only previous Thursday afternoon   14. 'Trends vary like the weather'   15a. Yes   15b. Yes, can be arranged   16. Only from known buyers   17. No rubbish   18. Varies from 1–4 weeks   19. £1–£500   20. Average 1,000 lots per month.

S. W. Cottee   2. The Market, East Street, **Wareham**, Dorset   3a. Regularly   3b. Occasionally   4. Local   5a. General—furniture and effects   5b. Specialist—monthly coin sales   6a. 15% furniture, 12½% coins   6b. None   7. Yes, if reasonable   8. No   9. No   10. Yes   11. Yes   12. Not known   13. Day before   14. Marked increase in antiques   15a. Furniture—No; Coins—Yes   15b. Can be arranged   16. Yes, if known   17. None   18. No   19. £5–£10   20. Good attendance at all sales, prices realised for antiques as good as any provincial saleroom.

Devon & Exeter Auction Galleries   2. Okehampton Street, **Exeter**, Devon   3a. Weekly   3b. Weekly   4. Devon   5a. Yes   5b. Yes, general antiques, silver, books, coins   6a. 12½%   6b. Nil   7. Yes, no sale, no commission   8. No   9. Yes   10. Yes   11. Yes   12. Tuesdays/Fridays   13. Day before   14. General sales show an upward trend of 40%, poor antiques down, better items up   15a. For better sales, yes; for general sales, lists   15b. No   16. Yes   17. Must be saleable   18. 7–21 days   19. Up to £50, 10% above   20. Fewer private buyers of antiques.

John Francis, Thomas Jones and Sons   2. Curiosity Sale Room, Queen Street, **Carmarthen**   3a. Every six weeks   3b. Periodically   4. West of the

Severn Bridge   5a. & b. General, rarely Specialist   6a. 12½%   6b. Nil   7. Yes, £1 on unsold lots   8. No   9. No   10. Yes   11. Yes, if known to us   12. Tuesdays   13. Afternoon before and prior to 10.30 on day   14. Dutch marquetry and oak showing an upward trend; watercolours down   15a. Yes   15b. By arrangement with carrier   16. Yes, with bankers' card   17. Do not take rubbish   18. Three weeks   19. All   20. Average of £16,000 worth per sale; auctioneers for 103 years; electric panel indicates what lot is being sold.

Hall, Waterbridge and Owen   2. Welshbridge, **Shrewsbury**; also at **Oswestry, Telford**   3a. Weekly   3b. When necessary   4. Salop and Border Counties   5. General   6a. 15% (special trade rate 10%)   6b. Nil   7. Yes, no charge for lots failing to reach reasonable reserve   8. No   9. No   10. Yes   11. Yes, if known   12. Fridays   13. Thursdays or by appointment   14. 1974 showed strong demand for longcase clocks, credenzas; eased in 1975; good and rising demand for all lots of quality   15a. Antique sales only   15b. Arranged through hauliers   16. Yes, bankers' references if unknown   17. None   18. Fortnight (household); up to six weeks (antiques)   19. Up to £50 for household, £1 upwards for antiques.

Charles Head & Son   2. 113 Fore Street, **Kingsbridge**, Devon   3a. Every 5 weeks   3b. Approx. 3 per annum   4. 10-mile radius of Kingsbridge   5a. & b. General   6. 15% up to £100 for single lots, 10% on single lots above £100; on owner's premises 7½% plus advertising and porterage disbursements   6b. No charge except VAT   7. Yes, subject to approval by our valuer   8. Never   9. Only with previous notice and in place of reserve   10. Yes   11. Yes   12. Thursdays   13. Day before   14. Notable upward trend in items of everyday use in Late Victorian and Edwardian times; e.g. flat irons, and kitchen utensils. Pinewood tables and chests have enormously increased in price; silver and jewellery have reached high prices. 1930s furniture is virtually unsaleable. Oak and mahogany Victorian furniture risen considerably   15a. No catalogues for sale rooms, but yes on private premises   15b. Arranged with outside firm   16. Yes, but sometimes have them verified before goods are released   17. Prams, beds, worn-out upholstery not accepted; otherwise anything reasonably saleable accepted   18. Goods accepted up to ten days before sale   19. £10–£50.

Humbert, Flint, Rawlence & Squarey   2. Furniture & Fine Arts Department, 8 Rollestone Street, **Salisbury**, Wilts   3b. As necessary, up to 3 per annum   4. Southern England   5a. & b. General   6a. 7½% plus expenses   6b. Nil   7. Yes   8. Not, repeat not, revealed   9. No   10. Yes, in writing   11. No   12. Thursdays   13. Day or days before   15a. Yes   15b. No   16. Yes, bank reference necessary   17. If up to standard, but *not* trade goods   18. N/A   19. N/A   20. No permanent sale room practice. Collective sales of a specialised nature undertaken in hired sale room.

King Miles & Co   2. The Square, **Axbridge**, Somerset   3a. & b. Premises at Town Hall, **Axbridge**; Bishops Barn, **Wells**   4. Avon & Somerset   5a. Yes, house clearances   5b. Mostly antique and Victoriana   6a. 12½% + VAT   6b. None   7. Yes, set by vendor, or vendor and auctioneer   8. Not usually   9. Yes   10. Yes   11. Yes, if full address given and person known   12. Last Friday in month   13. Afternoon on day prior to and morning of sale   14. Prices in 1974 were high and have fallen for average goods. Best quality goods continue to do well   15a. Yes   15b. will arrange on request   16. On producing bankers' card or full details prior to sale   17. No modern furniture   18. Entries up to two weeks before sale   19. £1–£500   20. Expanding fast and hope to increase number of sales next year.

Lalonde, Martin   2. 71 Oakfield Road, **Bristol** 8; Station Road, **Weston-super-Mare**   3a. Fortnightly   3b. Infrequently   4. Avon, South Gloucester and North Somerset   5a. & b. General   6a. 16% + 1% insurance   6b. None   7. 5% of reserve if not attained   8. No   9. Not usually   10. Yes   11. Only when confirmed in writing   12. Wednesdays—Bristol, Thursday—Weston-super-Mare   13. Day before   14. Prices have increased dramatically over the past two years, but are not tending to level off, with the exception of pictures which went over the top (like silver in the 1960s)   15a. Only for quarterly antique sales   15b. No   16. Yes, if supported by card or reference   17. All items are personally inspected before acceptance   18. Fortnightly, except when held for antique sale   19. General £10–£25 (average), Specialist £50–£100 (average)   20. Goods from the trade are not accepted

W. H. Lane & Son   2. Central Auction Rooms, **Penzance**, Cornwall   3a. Regularly   3b. 10–20 per annum   4. Southern England   5a. & b. General and Specialist   6a. 10% Specialist and antique, 15% household   6b. 5%   7. Yes, discussed with clients. Not usually a charge if reserve not reached   8. No   9. No   10. Yes   11. Yes   12. Not known   13. Not known   14. Goods between £200 and £1,000 have shown the biggest increases, silver and good furniture, including Victoriana, revived interest. 19th-century pictures have tended to fall   15a. Always   15b. Will arrange transport and delivery   16. If known, yes; if not, check with bank   17. No trade goods   18. All antiques within 6 weeks, pictures up to 2 months   19. £25–£200.

T. R. G. Lawrence & Son (Fine Art)   2. 19b Market Street, **Crewkerne**, Somerset   3a. Monthly   3b. Occasionally   4. South West   5. Specialist—all aspects in the fine art trade   6a. 15%   6b. None   7. Yes   8. No   9. —   10. Yes   11. Yes   12. Thursdays   13. Tuesday afternoon/Wednesday morning and afternoon prior   14. —   15a. Yes   15b. Yes   16. Only to known clients   17. Up to our standard   18. —   19. £25 upwards

Pearsons   2. Walcote Chambers, High Street, **Winchester**, and Fleet Road, **Fleet**, and 17 branches   3a. Approx. weekly   3b. 12 per annum   4. Southern Counties   5a. & b. General and Specialist (pictures and silver)   6a. 15%   6b. Nil   7. Yes, 5% charge if lot is unsold   8. Not usually   9. No   10. Yes   11. Yes, in *bona fide* cases   12. Tuesdays/Wednesdays/Thursdays   13. Day before 0930–1630   14. Finer antiques of every description have increased in price. Regency furniture, perfect porcelain are typical with rises of 100%   15a. Yes   15b. Can be arranged   16. Yes, from known purchasers, and from strangers if agreed   17. No electrical goods of any description; nor goods which are of a 'fringe' nature   18. Within four to six weeks   19. £25–£50   20. Broadly based business, covering landed property of all descriptions.

Harry Ray & Co 2. **Welshpool**, Mont. 3a. Monthly 3b. Periodically 4. Mid-Wales 5. General 6a. 15% 6b. None 7. Yes, if in writing 8. No 9. No 10. Yes 11. No, only in writing 12. Fridays 13. Thursday afternoons 14. 10% increase 15a. Yes 15b. Yes 16. Yes, with references 17. None 18. No 19. £10–£25 20. Deal in country antiques, including treen, farm tools and implements, Welsh dressers, clocks, etc. occasionally in silver and porcelain, prices up to £300.

Russell Baldwin & Bright 2. Ryelands Road, **Leominster**, Herefordshire 3a. Weekly 3b. Occasionally 4. Herefordshire and environs 5a. Yes, 3 times per month 5b. Yes, once a month 6a. 12½% over £100, 15% remainder 6b. Nil 7. A few, if agreed to be reasonable 8. No 9. Yes, occasionally 10. Yes, from prospective buyers 11. Yes, providing purchaser or buyer has inspected the goods 12. Thursdays 13. Wednesdays and morning of sales 14. Very appreciable upward trend in all sections, 100%–500% 15a. Yes 15b. Yes 16. Known customers or by arrangement with bank 17. Must be serviceable and saleable 18. 2–3 weeks for General, 4–6 weeks for Specialist 19. 50–60% up to £50 20. New saleroom in 1974; they now regard it as the best in the West; conduct almost all important art sales in the area. Almost all vendors private; trade *not* encouraged unless goods are exceptional.

Taviner's of Bristol (*Taviner's Auction Rooms*) 2. The Auction Rooms, Prewett St, Redcliffe, **Bristol** 3a. 7 or 8 per month 3b. Occasionally 4. Bristol and district 5a. Yes, every Friday (12 noon) 5b. Yes: antiques, first Thursday in the month; coins, third Friday in the month; books, third Friday in the month 6a. 16% 6b. Nil 7. Yes 8. No 9. No 10. Yes 11. Yes, confirmed in writing 12. As 5b 13. General: Sale day only; antiques: 3 days prior; books, coins: day of sale and day before 14. Late 19th- and early 20th-century rising by 33%+ over last eighteen months. Good coins up by 20%, general antiques depressed 15a. All, except gen. goods sales 15b. Arranged with outside contractors 16. Only with bankers' reference (maximum £30) or following banker's reference 17. Saleable 18. Three weeks at most 19. £50–£100, above £100 occasionally.

Ward & Chower 2. 1 Chard Lane, **Tavistock**, Devon 3a. No 3b. Public and private 4. West Devon and East Cornwall 5a. Yes 5b. Yes, sometimes books, prints, maps, silver and porcelain 6a. 15% 6b. None 7. Yes, no commission or expenses on unsold goods 8. No 9. Yes 10. Yes 11. No, unless client is well known to us 12. Wednesdays and Saturdays 13. Morning of sale and day prior 14. No significant trends noticed 15a. Yes 15b. Yes 16. Yes, if known or bank reference 17. Accepted up to week of auction 18. Week or so 19. £10–£25.

D. Ward & Son 2. 1 The Crescent, **Plymouth** 3a. Approx. quarterly 3b. When instructed 4. Devon and Cornwall 5. General but prefer to specialise in silver, plate and antiques 6a. 15% 6b. Nil 7. Yes, if satisfied they are realistic 8. No 9. Yes 10. Yes 11. Yes 12. Normally Thursdays 13. Day of sale 14. — 15a. Yes 15b. Can be arranged 16. Yes, on production of bankers' card 17. None 'providing they are what we require' 18. Yes in saleroom, depending on date of sale 19. Up to £100 20. A small auction room which is on the premises, therefore general household furniture not acceptable but silver, plate and smaller antiques preferred.

Wingett & Son   2. 29 Holt Street, **Wrexham**   3a. 10 per annum   3b. 6 per annum   4. North Wales, Cheshire & Salop   5. General   6a. $17\frac{1}{2}\%$ 6b. Nil   7. Yes, 10% buying-in charge   8. No   9. Yes   10. Yes   11. Yes   12. Wednesdays   13. Saturdays, Sundays (afternoon), Mondays   14. —   15a. Yes   15b. Yes   16. With bankers' reference   17. No dealer's stock   18. 1 month approx.   19. £50–£100   20. Apart from main Wrexham galleries have 25 sales per annum at their county saleroom, which are evening sales of Victoriana, Edwardiana and modern furniture and effects.

Midlands (inc. Cotswolds)

Barber & Son   2. 1 Church Street, **Wellington Telford**, Salop   3a. Monthly   3b. Irregularly   4. Shropshire   5a. & b. General   6a. $12\frac{1}{2}\%$ 6b. Nil   7. Yes, no charge   8. No   9. No   10. Yes   11. Yes, if known   12. Thursdays   13. Previous afternoon   14. —   15a. Only sales which are mostly antiques   15b. No   16. From people known, or need bankers' reference   17. Few   18. Not more than a month   19. Up to £500   20. Also sell houses so accept everyday furniture, which forms the basis of sales. No trade.

Blinkhorn & Co.   2. 41–43 North Street, **Broadway**, Worcs; 12 Vine Street, **Evesham**, Worcs   3a. Local Hall, approximately monthly   3b. Quarterly   4. North Cotswolds   5a. & b. Mostly General, some Specialist— silver, porcelain, clocks and table furniture   6a. 10% over £100, $12\frac{1}{2}\%$ £10– £100, 15% under £10   6b. None   7. Yes, 5% on top bid   8. No   9. No   10. Yes   11. Yes   12. Tuesdays   13. Monday prior   14. Early 19th century furniture rising greatly, very solid demand for classical pictures in good condition, very substantial increase (up to 300%) for copper and pewter   15a. Yes   15b. Arranged at vendor's cost   16. Yes, immediately   17. For general sales client's goods must average a minimum of £10 per lot   18. Yes, 2–3 months   19. Mostly £10–£50, but all others too.

E. J. Brooks & Son   2. Gloucester House, Beaumont Street, **Oxford**, also **Summertown**, **Banbury**, **Bicester**   3a. Fortnightly   3b. Occasionally   4. Oxfordshire, East Gloucestershire and North Berkshire   5a. & b. General mostly, Specialist—furniture, silver, pictures and ceramics   6a. $12\frac{1}{2}\%$ on £100+, $17\frac{1}{2}\%$ under £100, dealers charged $2\frac{1}{2}\%$ less in each case   6b. None   7. Yes, provided reasonable   8. Certainly NOT   9. Only up to reserve, if any   10. Yes   11. Yes   12. Fridays   13. Thursdays   14. Generally rising gradually, but pictures and water-colours down   15a. Yes   15b. By arrangement   16. Yes, with documentation   17. Must be saleable and unbroken   18. Maximum 6 weeks   19. £25–£50.

Buckell & Ballard   2. 1A Parsons Street, **Banbury**, Oxon.   3a. Approximately 20 sales per annum   3b. 4–5 times per annum   4. Oxfordshire, Berkshire, Buckinghamshire   5a. & b. General, occasionally Specialist   6a. 15% under £200, 12% individual lots £200–£500, 10% £500+   6b. Nil   7. Yes, no charge if their reserve   8. No   9. Rarely, but discouraged   10. Yes, i.e. commission to purchase at auction   11. Yes   12. Usually Tuesdays   13. Previous afternoon and evening and morning of sale   14. Generally continental furniture and early oak rising by 15% 15a. Yes 15b. Yes, arranged at vendor's cost 16. Yes, if known, otherwise goods held until cheque cleared 17. No domestic or bedroom effects unless whole house contents 18. 4–6 weeks general goods, 3–4 weeks better quality 19. £10–£50 20. Very little trade, mainly private vendors and estates.

Hall & Lloyd 2. 7 Church Lane, **Stafford** (telephone 4176) 3a. Every fortnight (alternate Thursdays) 3b. Yes, when contents of residence required to be sold 4. Stafford area 5a. & b. General only 6a. $12\frac{1}{2}$% 6b. Nil 7. Yes, small fee if many items unsold 8. Not before sale, sometimes afterwards 9. Yes 10. Yes 11. Yes, only from known clients 12. Alternate Thursdays 13. Wednesday afternoons prior 14. Edwardian pieces up 50% 15a. Only for special private sales 15b. Yes, by contract 16. Yes, with reference 17. Must be saleable 18. — 19. Most lots up to £5, but some up to £1,000.

Locke and England 2. 1 and 2 Euston Place, **Leamington Spa** 3a. Weekly 3b. When appropriate 4. Warwickshire and bordering counties 5a. & b. Household weekly, antiques monthly 6a. 15% 6b. None 7. No reserve if their recommendation. $2\frac{1}{2}$% if client's 8. No 9. No 10. Yes 11. Yes, only from established traders known to them 12. Thursdays 13. Day prior 14. — 15a. Yes 15b. Yes 16. From all *bona fide* buyers 17. Every item seen and vetted 18. 3–4 weeks 19. £10–£100 20. Discourage trade buyers: 'we have a good name as fair auctioneers selling "straight" goods.'

Mallam, Payne and Dean 2. Grosvenor Galleries, Grosvenor Street, **Cheltenham** 3a. Approximately 20 per annum 3b. Approximately 2 per annum 4. Cotswolds 5a. & b. General and Specialist—porcelain, paintings, furniture 6a. 15% 6b. Nil 7. Yes, by mutual agreement, no unsold charge 8. No 9. No option! 10. Yes 11. Under certain circumstances 12. Thursdays 13. 2 days prior to and morning of sale 14. Prices have remained steady over last 2 years 15a. Yes 15b. Yes 16. Yes, as normal 17. Antiques only 18. 3 weeks maximum 19. £1–£5,000.

Neal & Son 2. 155 Mansfield Road, **Nottingham**, NG1 3FR (telephone 0602 53511) 3a. Fortnightly 3b. Periodically, approximately 6 per annum 4. Nottinghamshire and Derbyshire 5a. & b. Fortnightly General sales, monthly Specialist—antique furniture, and 19th century furniture 6a. 11% for public or 10% for trade 6b. Nil 7. No charge on agreed reserve, otherwise 5% up to £100, $2\frac{1}{2}$% thereafter 8. No 9. No 10. No 11. If confirmed in writing 12. Thursdays 13. Tuesdays prior 14. General increase 15a. Yes 15b. Arranged by request 16. Yes, subject to bankers' reference 17. Saleability and acceptability of reserves 18. 1 week for general sales, 6 weeks for minority specialist items 19. General up to £50, Specialist £25–£1,000.

Phillips (in Knowle) 2. The Old House, Knowle, **Solihull**, West Midlands 3a. Weekly 3b. At intervals 4. Midlands, North, Wales and West 5a. & b. Specialist—antiques and fine art 6a. 15% 6b. None 7. Yes, after consultation with vendor 8. No 9. No 10. Yes 11. Yes 12. Wednesdays 11 a.m., evening wine sales 6.30 p.m. 13. Saturday

9 a.m. to 12 noon, Mondays and Tuesdays 9 a.m.–5 p.m., and morning of sale 14. — 15a. Yes 15b. Yes 16. To persons known or, if not, after consultation with bank 17. 4–8 weeks 18. All ranges 20. Branch of Phillips Son & Neale.

Henry Spencer & Sons 2. 20 The Square, **Retford**, Nottinghamshire 3a. 80–85 per annum 3b. 30–36 per annum 4. Scottish border down to a line through Oxford and Cambridge 5a. & b. Some General, mainly Specialist—furniture, works of art, models, porcelain, pictures, silver, coins, books, Victoriana 6a. $12\frac{1}{2}\%$ up to £20, $7\frac{1}{2}\%$ £20–£500, 5% £500–£10,000, $2\frac{1}{2}\%$ £10,000 6b. None 7. Yes, with $7\frac{1}{2}\%$ commission 8. No 9. No 10. Yes 11. Yes, if confirmed in writing 12. Tuesday–Fridays 13. Tuesdays, mornings of sale and some Saturdays 14. During last 2 years generally rising 20–25%, silver up 30%, paintings down dramatically during 2nd half of 1974 and early 1975—recovering well, but still below early 1974 levels 15a. Yes 15b. Yes, chargeable 16. Yes, with bankers' reference 17. None 18. Average 4–6 weeks 19. £5–£1,000.

Thimbleby's 2. Estate Office, Rose Farm, Rothefield Greys, **Henley on Thames**, Oxon 3a. 4 per month 3b. When required 4. Throughout the British Isles 5a. & b. Specialist only—china, pictures, coins, cigarette cards, post cards, stamps, oriental items 6a. $17\frac{1}{2}\%$ 6b. None 7. Yes, 5% unsold lots 8. No 9. No 10. Yes 11. Yes 12. Tuesdays/Thursdays 13. By appointment and day prior to selling including evenings 14. Generally downward in last year except for exceptional items 15a. Yes 15b. Yes 16. Yes 17. Only quality 18. 2–4 months 19. £10–£100.

Walker, Barnett & Hill 2. 3 Waterloo Road, **Wolverhampton** 3a. Quarterly 3b. Approximately monthly 4. West Midlands 5a. & b. General, and on own premises antique only 6a. 15% on own premises, 10% plus expenses on private premises 6b. Nil 7. Yes, free 8. No 9. Yes, he has a legal right to bid 10. Yes 11. Yes 12. Tuesdays/Thursdays 13. Day prior to and morning of sale 14. Rise in period oak 15a. Yes 15b. No 16. Yes, where payer known 17. Auctioneer's discretion 18. No 19. £100–£1,000 quarterly.

Warner, Sheppard & Wade 2. The Auction Mart, 16/18 Halford Street, **Leicester** 3a. Tri-weekly 3b. 3 or 4 per annum 4. Leicestershire 5a. & b. General 6a. 15% (books 20%) 6b. None 7. Yes, 5% if unsold on bought-in prices 8. No 9. No 10. Yes 11. Yes, but ask for confirmation 12. Mondays/Tuesdays/Wednesdays 13. Thursday, Friday and Saturday prior 14. Oak rising swiftly, now easing off; pictures eased off last six months; silver, porcelain, Victoriana still in demand 15a. Yes 15b. No 16. Yes, with bankers' reference 17. Must be saleable and not trade 18. Yes, maybe three months for better goods 19. £10–£25 20. Old firm with local family connections. General sales with classified sections every three weeks with a specially catalogued sale of higher quality items when sufficient material has accumulated.

Weller & Dufty Ltd 2. 141 Bromsgrove Street, **Birmingham** B5 6RQ 3a. 10 times per annum 3b. — 4. International 5a. & b. Specialist—arms, armour, militaria, etc. (especially modern sporting guns and firearms) 6a. 10–15% 6b. 5% 7. Yes, without restrictions 8. No 9. Yes 10.

Yes 11. Only if confirmed in writing 12. Tuesdays/Wednesdays 13.
Monday prior 14. General all round rise between 10% and 25% 15a.
Yes 15b. Yes 16. Covered by bank guarantee 17. None 18. Next
sale 19. a, b 21%; c, d, e 50%; f 8%; g $\frac{1}{2}$% of business.

London and Home Counties

W. & F. C. Bonham & Sons Ltd 2. Montpelier Galleries, Montpelier
Street, Knightsbridge, **London** SW7 3a. 6–8 times a week 3b. 3–4 times
a year 4. — 5a. & b. Specialist all areas 6a. 7% 6b. 10% 7. Yes 8.
No 9. Yes, but not on his own lots 10. Yes 11. Yes, from known
clients 12. Tuesdays, Wednesdays, Thursdays and Fridays 13. Normally two days prior unless otherwise stated 14. — 15a. Yes 15b.
Yes 16. Yes, from known clients, also other but goods cannot be cleared
before cheque 17. — 18. 3–5 weeks 19. £50–£1,000.
Chancellors & Co 2. 11 High Street, **Ascot**, Berkshire 3a. 8–10 per
annum 3b. When instructed 4. Wherever necessary 5a. & b. General
and Specialist—painting, porcelain and silver 6a. According to price
realised 6b. Nil 7. Yes, no sale, no fee (under review) 8. No 9.
No 10. Yes 11. Yes 12. 2nd Monday and Tuesday of month 13.
Friday and Saturday prior 14. Steady increase in all prices and subjects 15a. Yes 15b. Yes 16. Yes 17. Nil 18. 3 weeks 19. £50–£100.
Dreweatt, Watson & Barton 2. 22 Market Place, **Newbury**, Berks 3a.
Fortnightly at saleroom, **Northcroft**, Newbury 3b. About 20 a year 4.
Berkshire, Hampshire and Wiltshire 5a. & b. General once a month,
Specialist twice a year—silver, jewellery, pictures, books 6a. 15% under
£100, 12$\frac{1}{2}$% £100–£500, 10% over £500 6b. None 7. Yes, if owner
wishes, no buying-in fee 8. No 9. No 10. Yes 11. Yes, if known 12.
Wednesdays 13. Saleroom: day prior; private house: 2 days prior 14.
Prices have continued to rise owing to private buyers. Impossible to
estimate what good antiques will fetch 15a. Yes 15b. Arranged if
required 16. Yes, with safeguards, from strangers 17. Do not encourage
dealer's lots and refuse rubbish 18. 1 month 19. £25–£100 General,
£100–£1,000 Antique 20. Own staff of sale porters, sales broadly advertised.
A. C. Frost & Co 2. (opposite the station) **Beaconsfield**, Buckinghamshire
and 10 offices 3a. Never 3b. Only occasionally 4. South
Buckinghamshire, East Berkshire, North-West Surrey 5a. & b. General 6a. 10%–15% 6b. No 7. Yes 8. No 9. — 10. Yes 11. Yes, if
prospective buyer known 12. Wednesdays 13. Saturday and
Monday 14. Very few auctions in last 5 years, due mainly to rising value
of contents of most houses therefore most contents split up amongst
family 15a. Yes 15b. No 16. Yes, with identification 17. No rubbish 18. — 19. All prices 20. Estate agents first with auctioneering
service if required. No saleroom or regular sales.
J. Alexander Gunn Ltd 2. Wentworth Auction Galleries, **Virginia Water**,
Surrey 3a. Every 6–7 weeks 3b. 2–3 times a year 4. Virginia Water,
Surrey 5 a. & b. General 6a. 15% (private) 12$\frac{1}{2}$% (trade) 6b. Nil 7.
Accept reserves, charge 2$\frac{1}{2}$% on unsold lots if think reserve unreason-

able 8. No 9. No 10. Yes, but rarely happens 11. Yes, often 12. Usually Wednesdays 13. Day prior 9 a.m.–8 p.m. 14. No 15a. Yes 15b. Arranged 16. Yes, by prior arrangement 17. Must be saleable 18. No waiting time 19. £5–£10.

M. R. Harmer 2. 41 New Bond Street, **London** W1A 4EH 3a. Fortnightly, September–July 3b. — 4. London, New York, Sydney 5a. & b. Specialist—philatelic 6a. 12½%–20% 6b. None 7. Rarely and must be reasonable 8. No 9. Only by prior agreement 10. Yes 11. Yes 12. Monday–Wednesday 13. 2 or 3 days in previous week 14. Average increase in last two years 25% 15a. Yes 15b. Collection only 16. Yes, approved accounts 17. *Total* value at least £50 18. Around 4 months 19. Average £70–£80 20. Philatelic only.

Messenger, May, Baverstock 2. 93 High Street, **Godalming**, Surrey 3a. Antique every 4–6 weeks, General every 4 weeks 3b. When an auction arises 4. Any area, mainly south of England 5a. & b. General and Specialist—books, coins, paintings and furniture 6a. 15% 6b. Nil 7. Yes, no buying in fee if consider the reserves to be sensible 8. No, but an estimate will be given 9. No 10. Yes 11. Yes 12. Antique: Wednesdays/Thursdays; General: Saturdays 13. Usually 3 days prior 14. Prices generally increased by 20%–25%, paintings down by 30% 15a. Yes 15b. Yes 16. Yes, unless a large amount, then a bankers' reference 17. No trade, only from private houses or deceased estates, will sell nothing that has been in a dealer's shop on show 18. 1 month unless specialist, then 2–3 months 19. Average sale £50,000, average £55 per lot 20. Nothing is too much trouble or any article too small and are quite prepared to travel the breadth of this country.

Osenton's Auction Gallery 2. Milmead, **Guildford** and 15 branches 3a. Every three weeks 3b. When the opportunity arises 4. West Surrey and Hampshire 5a. & b. General 6a. 15% 6b. Nil 7. Yes, by agreement 8. No 9. No 10. Yes 11. Yes 12. Thursdays 13. Two days prior, Tuesdays 9 a.m.–1 p.m.; 2 p.m.–5 p.m., Wednesdays 9 a.m.–8 p.m. 14. Rise in demand for small items of value 15a. Yes 15b. Yes, by arrangement 16. Yes, if known or vouched for 17. Not less than £5 in value 18. Usually within three weeks 19. £10–£25 20. 'Ring us and ask' (0483 4030).

Phillips Son & Neale 2. 7 Blenheim Street, *London* W1Y DAS, also **Hayes Place**, NW (Thursdays), and Knowle, W. Midlands, Dowell's of Edinburgh 3a. 10 per annum 3b. Frequently, as advertised 4. Entire country 5. & b. General and Specialist 6a. 10% 6b. Nothing 7. Yes, 2½% if auctioneer's discretion, 5% if given by vendor 8. No 9. No 10. Yes 11. Yes 12. Send for list 13. On 2 days prior 14. — 15a. Yes 15b. By arrangement with contractors 16. Yes, by usual business arrangement 17. — 18. Not longer than 2–3 weeks, settlement within 2 weeks of sale 19. £50–£1,000. Send for booklet.

Pretty & Ellis 2. 19 Hill Avenue, **Amersham**, Bucks. Auction Room, 125 Station Road, **Amersham** 3a. Nearly every week 3b. — 4. Buckinghamshire 5a. & b. General 6a. 15% 6b. Nil 7. Yes, no terms first time offered for sale 8. No 9. Yes, providing no reserve 10. Yes 11. Yes 12. Thursdays 13. All day Wednesday and morning of sale 14.

General rise in price of all antiques and good quality reproduction furniture 15a. Yes 15b. Good contact with local removal firm 16. Yes, with bankers' card 17. Non-saleability 18. 4–6 weeks 19. Varies up to £1,000.

E. Reeves Ltd 2. 120 Church Street, **Croydon** 3a. Weekly for chattels 3b. Monthly (outside premises) for coins and medals 4. London and South East (chattels), worldwide (coins) 5a. & b. General and Specialist—coins 6a. Ask for entry form 6b. Nil 7. Yes, if unsold charge is $2\frac{1}{2}\%$ of reserve 8. On occasions before the sale 9. Yes 10. Yes 11. Yes 12. Mondays (chattels), Fridays (coins) 13. Friday and Saturday (for Monday), Thursday (for Friday) and mornings of sales 14. General increase for better quality antiques and coins 15a. Yes 15b. Can be arranged 16. Yes, by authority of a principal 17. Only saleable goods accepted 18. Included in next sale 19. £5–£10 (chattels), £10–£25 (coins).

Rosan & Co 2. 144–150 London Road, **Croydon**, Surrey 3a. Weekly 3b. Occasionally 4. Greater London and Surrey 5a. & b. General 6a. $12\frac{1}{2}\%$–20% (by arrangement) 6b. Nil 7. Yes, $2\frac{1}{2}\%$ if unsold 8. No 9. No 10. Yes 11. Yes 12. Saturdays 13. Friday prior and 1 hour before start of sale 14. — 15a. Yes 15b. Can be arranged 16. Yes, subject to bankers' references 17. — 18. No longer than 7 days 19. £5–£10.

Sotheby Parke Bernet & Co 2. 34–35 New Bond Street, **London** W1 3a. Everyday, September to July 3b. House sales, several a year 4. London (2 main offices), Scotland (e.g. Gleneagles) 5a. & b. General and Specialist (send for catalogues) 6a. 10% (6% dealers) 6b. 10% 7. Yes, see catalogues 8. No 9. No 10. Yes 11. Yes plus telegram to confirm (see catalogues) 12. Almost everyday 13. Several days in advance 14. — 15a. Yes, but they must be paid for 15b. Yes, but to be paid for by seller or buyer 16. Yes, with bankers' card 17. See catalogue 18. Yes, depends on department 19. Very wide ranging.

Tufnell & Partners 2. Estate Offices, London Road, **Sunninghill**, Ascot, Berks and 8 branches 3a. — 3b. As instructed 4. Berkshire, Surrey 5a. & b. General 6a. 15%, or to owner of principal contents $7\frac{1}{2}\%$ plus all costs 6b. No 7. Yes, no terms by arrangement 8. No 9. Yes 10. Yes 11. Yes 12. As instructed 13. One or two days prior 14. — 15a. Yes 15b. Carrier always in attendance 16. Yes, from buyers known 17. None 18. — 19. All prices, but £25–£100 principally 20. Chiefly surveyors and estate agents but deal in a large part with substantial country houses and consequently maintain an auctioneer and valuer.

West London Auctions 2. Lamertons Wreho, Sandringham Mews, W.5. 3a. Every two weeks (antiques and general alternately) 3b. — 4. Middlesex and West London. 5a & b. General and Antiques 6a. $12\frac{1}{2}\%$ (negotiable) to large trade vendors plus $\frac{1}{2}\%$ insurance plus 50p lot charge where practicable 6b. Not at present 7. $6\frac{1}{4}\%$ down to 0% 8. No 9. On prior agreement, charge if bought-in 10. Yes, entered in bids book 11. Yes, if bidder known, no large bid from unknown person 12. Wednesdays, 12.30 p.m. 13. General: day prior 5–7.30 p.m., day of sale 9.30 a.m.–12.30 p.m.; Antique: day prior 3–7.30 p.m., day of sale 10 a.m.–12.30 p.m. 14. Only opened March 1975 15a. Yes 15b. — 16. Very seldom, cash only 17. General: nothing dirty, and nothing which will involve sending a bill to vendor; Antique: vendor must give full particulars of himself and make a VAT statement. Aim for lot price of at least £10 average. Below this charge 50p per lot 18. General: maximum 2 weeks; Antiques: maximum 4 weeks.

The North (including Scotland)

Richard Baker & Baker 2. 9 Hamilton Street, opposite Hamilton Square Station, **Birkenhead** 3a. Fortnightly 3b. As and when appropriate 4. Merseyside and Wirral 5a. & b. General and Specialist—paintings, silver, porcelain and pottery, bronzes, ivories, glass, clocks, weapons, general Victoriana 6a. 15% 6b. None 7. Yes, at 5% charge on reserve price if lot unsold 8. No 9. No 10. No 11. Yes, if confirmed by telegram or letter 12. Mondays 13. Friday and Saturday prior 14. General upward trend, percentage difficult to determine 15a. Yes 15b. No 16. Yes, if supported by bankers' card or if from known customers 17. No trade goods or goods of low value 18. Two to four weeks 19. £10–£25.

Boulton & Cooper Ltd 2. Forsyth House, **Malton** 3a. Approx. twice a month 3b. Approx. twice a month 4. North and East Yorkshire 5a. & b. General 6a. Negotiable 6b. None 7. No (no charge for unsold lots) 8. No 9. — 10. Yes 11. Yes, if bidder known or a local 12. Wednesdays, Thursdays (Saturdays if on vendor's premises) 13. Day before 14. — 15a. Yes, for antique sales only 15b. Occasionally 16. Yes, depends on buyer 17. — 18. 1 month 19. Up to £5 (house clearing), £25–£100 (antiques—some over £1,000).

Messrs Dee & Atkinson 2. The Exchange, **Driffield**, East Yorkshire and 14 North Bar, **Within**, Beverley, Yorkshire 3a. — 3b. — 4. — 5a. & b. General 6a. 12½%–15% 6b. None 7. Yes 8. No 9. No 10. Yes 11. Yes 12. Fridays 13. Two afternoons prior 14. More demand for genuine goods 15a. Yes 15b. If needed 16. Only with bankers' references 17. — 18. 4 weeks 19. £10–£50.

Dowell's 2. 65 George Street, **Edinburgh** EH2 2JL 3a. 2–3 per week 3b. As requested 4. All Scotland, and access to international markets *via* Phillips in London 5a. & b. General household each Thursday, Specialist majority 6a. 15% (12% trade) 6b. None 7. Occasionally, 5% buying-in fee 8. No 9. — 10. Yes 11. No 12. Send for list 13. 2 days prior 14. Generally steady upward trend especially in quality articles; oil paintings and Scottish silver up most 15a. Yes 15b. Independent contractor 16. Yes 17. Quality must be reasonable 18. Ten days to three weeks 19. £10–£100 20. Associated to Phillips in London; specialists in all departments.

G. H. Edkins & Son 2. 122 Newgate Street, **Bishop Auckland**, Co. Durham 3a. Fortnightly 3b. Occasionally 4. North East 5a. & b. General 6a. 15% (10% to trade) 6b. 5% 7. Yes 8. During sale 9. No 10. Yes 11. Yes, from people known 12. Thursdays 13. Wednesdays 14. Increase generally overall 15a. Yes, for better sales 15b. Yes 16. Yes, if known or with bankers' card   17. None   18. Two weeks   19. Up to £100.

Laidlaws   2. Crown Court Auction Mart, **Wakefield** WF1 2SU, also at **Castleford** and **Normanton**   3a. 6 sales per annum   3b. Very few   4. 10 miles of Wakefield   5a. & b. Specialist—antiques   6a. 15% plus VAT   6b. Nil   7. Yes, 10%–7½% if unsold   8. No   9. No   10. Yes   11. Yes   12. Wednesdays (and also Thursdays on two-day sales)   13. Saturday and Tuesday previous, trade only Monday   14. General upward trend all round   15a. Yes   15b. No   16. Yes   17. No trade goods   18. Yes, depending on date of sale   19. £5–£20 bric-à-brac, £25–£100 furniture.

Morrison McGhlery & Co   2. 98 Sauchiehall Street, **Glasgow** G2   3a. 2 per week   3b. Occasionally   4. —   5a. & b. General and Specialist—antiques, pictures, silver, jewellery, coins, stamps, books   6a. Up to 15%   6b. Nil   7. Occasionally, 5% buying-in fee   8. No   9. No   10. Yes   11. Yes, with confirmation   12. Tuesdays and Thursdays   13. Day before and morning of sale   14. Steady increase of approximately 25% per annum   15a. Yes   15b. Sometimes   16. If known   17. Must be saleable   18. 1 day to 30 days   19. £25–£50.

Alfred Massop & Co   2. Compston Road, **Ambleside**, also **Kendal**   3a. Every three weeks   3b. Occasionally   4. Lake District   5a. & b. General   6a. 17½%   6b. None   7. Yes, though reluctantly   8. No   9. No   10. No   11. Yes, if known to us   12. Saturdays commencing 10 a.m.   13. Three days prior, 9 a.m.–5.30 p.m.   14. Small antiques, jewellery, objets d'art rose enormously in last 2 years   15a. Yes   15b. Yes   16. Yes, bankers' card if not known   17. Conditions on entry form   18. Continuous process, sales every three weeks   19. £5–£100   20. Sell very little on behalf of trade, but have many trade buyers.

Outhwaite & Litherland   2. Kingsway Galleries, Fontenoy Street, **Liverpool** L3 2BE   3a. 7 per month   3b As and when available   4. North-West England   5a. & b. General, Specialist—all aspects of Fine Art   6a. 10%–18% according to value and type, photography and insurance free   6b. 5%   7. Yes, 5% on unsold   8. No   9. Not encouraged   10. Goods never sold privately prior to auction but bids may be left with porters   11. Yes, with subsequent express confirmation   12. Tuesdays (weekly), Wednesdays (fortnightly and monthly)   13. At least a day prior   14. Prices much increased over the last 2 years, excluding pictures. In pictures really good artists and Victorian pictures have come into their own   15a. Yes, for Fine Art sales   15b. Yes, at an extra charge   16. Yes, must be verified or cleared   17. Quality and condition must be high enough for inclusion in Fine Art sales. These 98% from private sources   18. 1 month Fine Art, General immediately   19. £5–£1,000   20. Trade goods not usually accepted.

Thomas Skidmore & Son   2. Imperial Chambers, 47 Lichfield Street, **Wolverhampton**   3a. Every Friday (excluding Bank Holidays)   3b. Occasionally as requested   4. West Midlands   5a. & b. General, Specialist by request   6a. 15%   6b. Nil   7. Yes, nominal charge, reserve usually placed after discussion   8. No, but if item unsold might be discussed with prospective purchaser   9. No   10. Yes, but do not sell prior to sale   11. Yes, usually from people known   12. Every Friday   13. Every Thursday   14.

All items rising due to inflation, antiques particularly 15a. Yes 15b. Yes, reasonable charge 16. Yes, from those known, but now *never* from strangers 17. If saleable and reserves not too high 18. 7 days unless retained for special sale 19. Mostly £0–£10. Max. (seldom) £1,000.

Louis Taylor & Sons 2. Percy Street, **Hanley**, Stoke-on-Trent 3a. Weekly 3b. As instructed, perhaps four times a year 4. — 5a. & b. General, Specialist quarterly—mixed antiques 6a. 15% 6b. Nil 7. Only approved and reasonable reserves 8. No 9. No 10. Yes, i.e. commissions from buyers 11. Yes 12. Mondays 13. Friday and Saturday prior 14. Distinct rise in all sections over past 2 years 15a. For special sales 15b. Arranged by us 16. Yes, but require evidence from bank for new customers 17. Do not accept unsaleable lots and lots with too high reserves 18. Two weeks up to sale (except antiques), and up to 2 weeks for cheques 19. £10–£50, often £1,000+ 20. General auction room business for nearly 100 years and specialise both in general good class furniture and effects, and also in General Fine Art special sales.

James Thompson 2. 64 Main Street, **Kirkby**, Lonsdale, and **Settle** and **Garstang** 3a. Monthly 3b. 3 or 4 times per annum 4. South Lakeland, North Yorkshire, Yorkshire Dales 5a. & b. General and Specialist—3 pictures per annum, several sales with silver section each year 6a. 15½% 6b. Nil 7. Yes, on agreed reserve no sale, no fee 8. No 9. Prefer a fixed reserve 10. No 11. Only if confirmed in writing 12. Wednesdays 13. Tuesday 9.30 a.m.–3 p.m. 14. Silver rising sharply, especially quality Victorian. Most antique furniture rising, paintings not rising until recently 15a. Only for picture sales 15b. Arranged if required 16. Yes, with bankers' reference if unknown 17. Subject to inspection, not generally trade 18. 4 weeks 19. c, d, e and f.

Two: Antiques Fairs

Grace is given of God, but knowledge is bought in the market-place.

Arthur Hugh Clough

Everybody's doing it. It's sweeping the country. In some places they do it for charity, in others for greed. The AA and RAC put up signs to help you find them at it and even the Bucks Education Committee is sponsoring it in some of their schools. In some places they do it in the afternoons, elsewhere in the evenings. Some do it out-of-doors, though I prefer doing it sheltered from the elements; I don't like getting my things covered in smut.

I refer of course to the Antiques Fairs.

Not that they always call them that. They can be called collectors' markets, bazaars or even junk-hunts. Sometimes they give

them such fancy names as Trash and Treasure, or Granny's Attic, or Collectormania. Usually they are non-specialist, but Bolton has its giant Flea-Market and Autojumble, Cheltenham its very own Arms and Militaria Fair, and Southampton its Southern Counties Grand Christmas Bottle Festival and Auction. Whatever they call them they are taking over from shops and auction rooms as the most convenient, enjoyable and economical way of bringing together the man with the wallet and the man with what the man with the wallet wants. More often than not, it's not a man at all, but a woman or women who organise and run these events, and increasingly now it's a company. There's Silhouette Fairs and there's Step-In Markets, there's Porter and Addy, and Whatnot Fairs. To give some idea of the extent of the phenomenon, on a typical recent Saturday there were antique fairs recorded at Caversham, Westerham, Wigan, Darlington, Harrow, Peterborough, Skegness, Pontefract, Bakewell, Braintree, Southport and Richmond, while on the Sunday following you could find them at Ruislip, Hartley Wintney, Aston Clinton, and the American Air Force Base, Upper Heyford. So rapidly are they mushrooming that it's extremely difficult to provide an up-to-date list, but *Collector's Bazaar* (published by Abbey Publications, 14 Broadway SW1—01-834 9225) does its best, and *Exchange and Mart*, the nanny of them all, includes, under its 'Collectors' heading, advertisements for a good cross-section of fairs, and the telephone numbers of the organisers should you wish to take a stall.

The Grosvenor House, Hilton, Earl's Court and Chelsea Fairs in London are sufficiently grand to justify exclusion in a modest work such as this one; few of their goods carry anything as vulgar as a price ticket, sums of money are exhaled in reverential tones with lowered eyelashes and clearings of throats, and you'll not find many bargains there, although a visit to any one of them is a feast to the eye. I visit them but rarely, finding too acute the pain of spotting a cup and saucer indistinguishable from one I sold on my stall for a couple of pounds displayed like the Crown Jewels on a velvet cushion.

The true bargain hunter makes instead for the Welfare Hall, Goldthorpe, or the Scout Hut, Chalfont St Giles, or the Penistone Cinema, Leeds or even the Members Enclosure at Ascot Race Course, where Sundays are given over to horses of a very different colour.

You should not be scared to visit such places, and, if the sound of an 'antiques and collectors' fair' affrights you, rest assured that you'll not find many genuine antiques there—a genuine antique has to be at least a hundred years old according to the British Antique Dealers Association (who ought to know)—but you will find a great many items most moderately priced.

The fairs work like this. Between twenty and sixty dealers will be invited to take stalls and will pay between £4 and £20 for the privilege. This money entitles them to a six-foot trestle table plus enough floor space in front of it to set up smaller coffee table displays and enough space behind it to hang pictures or mirrors or clothes. In my experience people prefer to buy from the periphery of my stall (around the side, under the skirts of the tablecloth, in boxes etc.) fancying perhaps that, while the grander items are on public view, the true treasures require excavation. Good luck to these brave speleologists; they usually earn their rewards, hunting through a morass of model cars to find the Dinky Toy they need to complete their collection, thumbing through piles of picture postcards for the Dorset agricultural scene or the Steyning postmark or whatever it is that sets their blood coursing through their veins.

You may be charged up to 50p for admission, which entrance money is sometimes given to charity—or admittance may be free. There will always be refreshments available, quiches or a ploughman's lunch or a cheesy baked potato. The stall-holders assemble from eight in the morning (in the case of a day-time fair) and unload their stock from a conglomeration of Land-Rovers, estate-cars and vans. And directly in their wake come the scavengers. When Yvonne and I unpacked the goods for our first-ever stall at the Castle Hotel, Richmond, the air around our pitch was black with carrion sniffing us out, hovering over each treasure which we displayed and plummeting down to feed greedily upon the tasty carcases of our ignorance. Not that we cared. We were flattered; and put our popularity down to our business acumen.

But it's not essential to be up alert and early on such occasions. For one thing it's much simpler to spy out the stock when the crowds are not so dense and for another, if you happen by at the end of the market (usually around 4 pm) stall-holders are far keener to drop the prices of their goods than they might have been earlier in the day. A late sale means a little more profit and a little less packing: tempting; very tempting. Under such circumstances a 50% discount is not unheard of.

And while on the subject of bargaining, do. Most stall-holders work on 100% mark-up which means in effect that they'll accept considerably less than the marked price. Some code their price tickets, the code relating to the trade price available; others put on specific goods N/T, signifying No Trade. Yes, bargain by all means, but respect the right of the stall-holder *not* to drop his prices if he chooses not to. Usually such obduracy indicates that in the opinion of the vendor the item really *is* worth the marked price and that he can certainly get such a price in due course. Sometimes when I refuse to drop the price it is because the object appeals particularly to me. A malicious brass bird, unlike any specimen known to ornithologists, used to leap from his perch on my stall on to any fragile china or glass which he could spy. Nonetheless his charm was such that I refused to reduce his price below £1·50, and now he preens himself on top of my television and perches on the indoor aerial. I *know* that my set of four white and gilt French oyster plates are worth £10 and have so far refused to bargain. How long can I go on like this?

At many antiques fairs there is one section devoted to objects brought in and priced by their owners. An excellent idea. For those without the time or the energy to take a stall of their own, it is possible to leave a few treasures at the beginning of the day, and call in later to check whether sales have been forthcoming. The organisers keep 15% or 20% commission, nor is this simple greed; they have to hire people to supervise the stall. If you are in doubt about what price to put on your things, inquire and the organiser or supervisor will be sure to suggest a fair price.

What sort of goods are likely to sell? The second part of this book may give you some hints on those areas in which you might like to specialise, and there is plenty of choice.

There are those who neither take a stall for themselves, nor leave their goods to be sold on commission by the organisers, but bring round to the stall-holders little carrier bags stuffed with treasures. One familiar face at antiques markets is a youngish man with plastic sandwich boxes full of small silver items. Where he gets his supplies from is mysterious, but he evidently buys very cheap indeed since he is able to sell to stall-holders at prices low enough for them too to make a profit. Another man dresses like a tramp (for all I know he is a tramp) and produces from the ragged linings of his clothes old war-medals and coins, which he buys from jumble sales (q.v.). His demeanour is so pathetic that I find myself (as I'm sure others do) paying above the odds for his goods and selling him run-down watches, which he claims to be able to repair, for twenty-five pence. A man who evidently knows what he is about. At other times I've been offered books and china and furniture and pictures; I've had a predatory housewife suggest that I might like to 'have a look at my things in case there's anything you fancy', and a pensioner offer his grandfather's silver half-hunter.

If you decide to offer things to stall-holders, don't take the first offer you receive. Shop around. You will find that the offers vary significantly, and of course you're entitled to take the best. If I'm offered something of real quality or obvious value by somebody who clearly doesn't appreciate what they have got, I usually suggest that they take the goods along to their nearest auctioneers.

But if you decide to take a stall on your own account here's what has to be done. Having approached the organiser you will most likely find that stalls are available for the next scheduled fair. You will be told that they've been booked out for weeks, that there's a long waiting list, that it's lucky you asked at just that moment, because only a few minutes before an unlucky cancellation . . . and so on. You are not generally required to pay in advance, although, if it is to be your first stall, it might be politic to offer to do so. You may be asked what sort of goods you specialise in; there are fairs which impose a dateline. These range from the six-day Scarborough fair, appropriately sited at the Grand Hotel, which accepts only goods dating from pre-1860 to several (Ashbane, Cleethorpes, Matlock etc.) with a dateline of 1940. Such occasions tend to be more like trade conventions than public markets and should be avoided by beginner and bargain-hunter alike.

If you decide to take a regular stall in a fair or fairs, you will need transport. I was particularly lucky in acquiring for £40 an ex-GPO Morris van. This is large enough to take all my stock plus small items of furniture and has always been reliable. An estate-car or any model with fold-down back-seats, or a large boot, will probably be adequate, and, should you specialise in small items, such as jewellery or coins, you can surely manage with whatever you normally drive. There are dealers who come in taxis and hired pantechnicons, but anything which adds to your overheads is to be discouraged. You will also need somewhere to store your stock; a box-room or cellar is ideal, or you can lock it permanently in your transport if you are prepared to risk it being stolen.

What else will you need? A table-cloth for your stall is essential and it should be one attractive enough to set off the goods without being so elaborately patterned as to distract the eye. Glass looks best on a white cloth, unless it is engraved, in which case a black background is best. Black also flatters jewellery, gold and silver. A coffee table, preferably collapsible or with screw-on feet, is useful for setting up in front of your stall, giving additional display space. Plate-hangers and stands (available from D. C. Monk and Co., 132 Church Street, Kensington; Mortlake Antiques, 69 Lower Richmond Road, Mortlake, London SW14 7HJ; Alan Morris (Wholesale), 503 Evesham Road, Crabbs Cross, Redditch, Worcs; or Lenham (Import and Export) and Co., Rottingdean, Sussex BN2 8AH) are obviously helpful if you have plates for sale, and display cabinets, open dressers, cake stands, miniature chests and footstools can all be used to give visual interest to your goods. A stall which is entirely on a horizontal plane is tiresome, and always bear in mind that your customers will be looking down on your stall. Lateral thinking can be carried too far.

Bring along a tin in which to keep the takings, a pad on which to record the sales, a couple of pounds worth of change for the early part of the day, a tea-cloth, soapy water in a bottle, metal and silver polish, a magnifying glass and a thermos of hot coffee with a packet of sandwiches. Also a good book in case business is bad, for nothing is more wretched than being without either customers or occupation.

Here, to save time, is Yvonne's list in toto, which she collated in the early days of our stalling.

2 tablecloths
Tin for receipts, float and note-paper
Thermos
Candles
Sellotape
Labels
String
Rubber bands
Newspaper for wrapping
Carrier and paper bags
Carpet
Radio
Dog basket
Finger-gloves
Hat
Display stand (stool and table)
Velvet box/cushion

A few words of explanation. The candles are for additional light in the event of the hall being under-lit. They also make glass sparkle and china glow. The carpet and the dog-basket are for the dog (now happily dogs) to lie on and in. The radio for Desert Island Discs and the racing results. The finger-gloves are to avoid the grime which handling newspapers invariably involves, and the velvet box/cushion is for pinning pieces of jewellery to. What the hat is for I've no idea. I can't remember: no more can Yvonne.

Three: Charity Shops and Jumble Sales

As a cousin of mine once said about money, money is always there but the pockets change; it is not in the same pockets after a change, and that is all there is to say about money.

Gertrude Stein

It is a law of nature that you cannot expect to find a bargain in opulent surroundings. Out of the dead caterpillar crawls the butterfly; out of the putrescent lion came the honey. Similarly you have no justification for complaining to the Bond Street dealer that you've seen a cabinet just like his at half the price back home in Betwys-y-Coed. He will tell you, if he is a man of spirit, which, having progressed as far as Bond Street he is likely to be—that back home in Betwys-y-Coed they don't pay comparable rates, nor employ ex-public-schoolboys to take your money, nor keep security agents on tap, nor display their treasures in such wide open spaces that each necklace could be around the neck of an heir to the throne, so uncontaminated is it by the hustling presence of cruder gewgaws.

The corollary to this ought to be that the grubbier the environment the more startling the bargain available. Ought to be, but ain't. There are shop-keepers not a thousand miles from the raucous public library in which I write these words (and the librarians are the noisy ones, not the public who are good as gold) who resolutely set about providing just such squalor in order that simple yokels from the West End shall be deceived.

And this is the moment to give common sense its head. Common sense requires that the lower the overheads the retailer must pay, the lower the price he needs to charge. There are other variables, such as the x factor (the ignorance of the dealer concerned), but this

Law of Overheads is basic. And the lowest overheads of all are enjoyed by jumble-sales, charity-shops and thieves.

So far as this last class is concerned, it can be unwise to do business with them. A sweet old gentleman, who used to run a weekly stall at Surbiton Assembly Rooms (where one does not expect Life to play such boisterous tricks), was one Friday no longer there, and in his place a burly inspector, cap in hand, and somewhat embarrassed by so many vulnerable items laid out in such a cavalier display.

'Did you purchase anything,' he asked each one of us in turn, 'from the gentleman who used to have a stall in that corner?' And shamefacedly one dealer after another was forced to cough up this or that little item which glinted wickedly in the artificial light.

But so far as jumble sales and charity shops are concerned, anything goes. I spoke to the shop organisers at the four charities principally concerned with running shops, Oxfam with 580 in the UK, Help The Aged with 55, War On Want with 35, and Shelter with, as the devolutionary lady intriguingly put it, 'seventeen shops in the United Kingdom and four in Scotland'. This is big business. Oxfam estimates the annual turnover from its shops as being somewhere in the region of three million pounds. But though there are bargains to be had in the charity shops, surprisingly it is not always intended that there should be. The man from Help The Aged in Hastings (the organisation is based in Hastings; I wouldn't want you to think that it is only the lucky aged in Hastings who are helped) was uncompromising:

'Anyone who comes into one of our shops and buys a bargain, we've failed.' Did he really mean that? He insisted that he did. 'If people donate articles to us, it's our job to get the full price for them, £10 for an article worth £10. If I mark it down to £5, the general dealers who look in our shop windows twice a day would snap it up. We run our business on business lines. We always have a paid manageress in every shop with a stockbook and a salesbook in which every item of fifteen pence and upwards is entered, the money is banked daily, and the shops are open from 9.30 to 5.00 pm every day.'

Shelter on the other hand employs entirely voluntary helpers who can claim expenses but nothing more except a clear conscience. Consequently you should have a better chance of finding a bargain in a Shelter shop than in a Help The Aged shop.

War On Want specialises in second-hand clothing, which is sen-

sible of them, since they find they can obtain and sell that commodity more easily than anything else.

'Now people know what things are worth,' the War On Want lady said sadly, 'they tend to sell them to antique dealers rather than bring them to us.' I blushed under my tan. War On Want prices goods according to the siting of their shops. 'The prices in our Portobello Road shop are lower than in our Ealing or Finchley Road shops, for instance. But nothing is ever priced at more than £15.'

Oxfam employs both voluntary and expert help (so does War On Want), with a pricing committee which will call on local traders where necessary (so does War On Want), and even on occasion National Museums and Famous Pundits. Help The Aged has travelling area managers to help price the better items, while Shelter ('most of our stuff is well-worn, but we did once sell a fur coat for £27') do all the pricing themselves.

It's obviously no longer as easy for the charity shops as it once was. The special rating concessions for charities were removed in 1974—the matter was taken to the House of Lords, but the Noble Lords were unmoved—and it is increasingly difficult for the shops to come by good quality gifts. They are not legally permitted to buy anything for resale, although most of them have registered trading companies to buy on their behalf. But you should certainly not ignore your local charity shops in your search for bargains, and, if you find a bargain there is no reason to feel guilty about snapping it up; if you don't somebody else will. However it might be an idea to celebrate your percipience with a donation of your own. The shops tell me that they will accept anything (except firearms, which are Not Allowed). 'Rather than upset anyone by turning their gifts away,' said the lady from War On Want, 'we take the rubbish in at the front door and out at the back!'

Charity shops are amiable and agreeable places where you may safely graze. Not so jumble sales. At a typical jumble sale modest and godfearing Mothers of Five are reduced to ravening beasts, and strong men to tears. It is an awful thing to see a man cry at a jumble sale. And yet it is at jumble sales that the greatest bargains are to be found, and there are antique dealers whose supply of antiques emanates almost entirely from that source. But you need to be spry. If you are not through the doors of that church hall within the first few minutes, all you will be left with are remnants (which is not to say that you won't find a few tasty morsels). And hence the

difficulty. In my area of Richmond and Twickenham, nine out of ten jumble sales are held on Saturdays, and eight out of ten on Saturday afternoons. Most of these open their doors between two o'clock and three. Parking facilities tend not to exist. Even on a Yamaha you will find it hard to get in at the start of more than two or three. Many jumble sales specialise in old clothes, in local produce, in home-made handicrafts, and in modern books; these are useless to your serious bargain-hunter, and he will have wasted time attending them, and queued up to get in, and paid 2p admittance most likely; he will not be best pleased. But should there be a bric-à-brac stall he will sniff it out like a police dog on the prowl for drugs, and make straight for the cutlery tray. Pieces of silver masquerading as plate can frequently be found at jumble sales, and since silver can be scrapped at £3 per ounce, it's no wonder that the cutlery tray is an attraction. Although the prices at jumble sales are no longer as ludicrously inadequate as they once were (the stuff is there to be got rid of in less than a day; it's a good cause, and nobody has time to examine the goods in detail) you will not often be asked to shell out more than 50p. Items at one and two pence are still the rule rather than the exception, and it's most unusual to find nothing of interest, even at that modest price.

Etiquette at jumble sales requires that you should not conduct lengthy negotiations with the harassed and over-worked helpers. If you've found your bargain pay the full price for it with a good grace and, if possible, the correct change. Nor is it reasonable to ask for items to be kept for you, or gift-wrapped, or wrapped at all, so bring with you a deep shopping bag and plenty of newspaper.

Where do you find your nearest jumble sales? Local papers are the most productive source of information, but you will also find jumble sales advertised on church notice boards, in newsagents windows, in the 'Sell-Out' section of *Time Out*, and in the pages of the parish magazine.

Four: London Street Markets

There are two fools in every market: one asks too little, one asks too much.

Russian proverb

For those who remember with nostalgic regret the camaraderie of war-time service life, or for those who stayed at home to enjoy the bombings and the queues, for those who jived away the fifties and for the children of the sixties who discovered at free pop festivals that many a warm heart beat under an embroidered smock before the petals of flower-power wilted, the street market offers the nearest thing to gaiety that these stern seventies can provide. Most cities of any consequence can boast at least one such market and some of them, such as Paddy's Market in Liverpool, are less a market than a community festival. You will find in the next chapter a list of the principal street markets in the principal towns and cities of the UK, but here I recommend to you some of the street markets of London, which still offer scope for junkard and serious collector alike.

For a comprehensive guide to London's street markets I should suggest dipping into Jeremy Cooper's book *The Complete Guide to London's Antique Street Markets* (Thames and Hudson, 1974) at £3·50, from which I have borrowed more perhaps than he might have been willing to lend. Mr C. concentrates on the three major markets of Portobello, Camden Passage and Bermondsey, but there is also an astonishing range and empiricism of London open markets.

1. The Big Guns
If you can build a business up big enough, it's respectable.

Will Rogers

Portobello Road

You can't count the number of stall-owners and shop-keepers who foregather in the Portobello Road early every Saturday; they won't stand still. But most estimates reckon on at least 2,000. If every stall-holder has five hundred articles, then you have a million possibilities of making a killing. But you'll be lucky if you do. Prices are as high as at any market in London and some dealers reckon to add 40% to the going rate when they take a stall in the Portobello Road, especially during the summer months. The southern end of the market is the posh end, but to the north of the market, above (or below if you're Australian) the fruit and vegetable stalls, things become less grand, the stall-holders younger, the objects less venerable, the atmosphere less sacerdotal. Also clustered to the south of the Westbourne Grove crossroads are the majority of the arcades, but should you chance your arm and pioneer as far as Golborne Road you will find an altogether junkier scene, much as Portobello Road used to be when collecting was a pastime and not a mania; and if, greatly daring, you make it to the Westway Flyover, you will find a market run by the North Kensington Amenity Trust, which is open on Fridays as well as Saturdays, and in which—the stall-holders being newer to the business—you are most likely to find your bargain.

The times of the Westway market are 8 am to 5.30 pm, Friday and Saturday, while Portobello's official hours are 8.30 am to 5.30 pm, Saturdays only. I say official hours advisedly, because the stall-holders will arrive considerably earlier, and, as soon as their stalls are up, they will be more than happy to do business with you. And should you arrive in the last hour of official business you may well find little more than litter, empty boxes, chips of china and shattered glasses.

I think a word of warning might be appropriate here. Portobello can be very seductive. So many people clustered around the stalls, so much stuff, so much bargaining and hassling, it's easy to be carried away. I'm a chess player and in a big match I try to remember to sit on my hands to ensure that I take a moment to study the position before making what appears to be an inspired move. At Portobello Market you would do well to keep your wallet or cheque book buttoned away in an inside pocket. This will not only secure you against pickpockets (a real danger in the bustle of the market) but will ensure that you stop to consider: 'Is this *really* cheaper than I could buy it in a shop?', 'Do I *really* like this?', 'Am

I *sure* it's what I want?' before plunging in. I have bought a bargain in the Portobello Road (a charming primitive painting of a huge bull in a flowery field) but it was many years ago, and competition was not so fierce.

No; Portobello is not for me. But if it is for you, then take a No 7, 15 or 32 bus or any bus or tube that takes you to Notting Hill Gate, whence you must walk up Pembridge Road. But please, I beg you, don't try to drive up Portobello Road. It's as foolhardy as taking your kitten to Crufts, and may well have been banned entirely by the time this book is in your hands.

If you would like to take a stall in the Portobello Road, you need to make your enquiries to the Senior Street Inspector, Haydens Place Sub Depot, Haydens Place, London W11 (01-727 8114). He will tell you that there is a five year waiting list, but you need not despair. Stalls in the various indoor arcades are readily available (go along and ask) and advertisements regularly appear in the *Evening Standard* classified columns, giving the number to ring for a stall. Alternatively if you would like to try your luck in the friendly and less formal atmosphere of the Westway Market you should contact the North Kensington Amenity Trust, 3 Acklam Road, W10 (01-969 7511). They are likely to welcome you.

New Caledonian Market (Bermondsey)

Before the last war (you'd be too young to remember) the Caledonian Market was to be found in Camden Town. Its comparatively new premises (Bermondsey Square) and appalling business hours (Friday, officially from 7 am to 2 pm, but in practice from 4.30 am) are intended to discourage the tourist, for this is the professionals' market, the only open air market in London which is devoted to the Antiques Trade and nothing else. Inevitably, this exclusivity has acted as a spur to the sightseer (it's a syndrome— who would want to look at those tedious old Pompeii doodles if the Pompeians hadn't put it about that they were filthy and that women and children and persons of a nervous disposition would not be permitted to view them?) so that the Caledonian dealers are no longer left alone to make profits and fools out of one another.

The Bermondsey Market is pleasant enough on a fine, summer's morning, birdsong, the smell of freshly baked bread, curly-headed urchins hurling bricks at passers-by; but to experience its sado-masochistic delights to the full, make your way there in midwinter.

By five o'clock things are beginning to hum. Trestles are erected with magical dispatch and already the mobile canteen is doing a roaring trade in hot dogs (with mustard and onions, natch!) and tea and coffee. Regulars bring hand-torches with them and the goods displayed on the crepuscular stalls glow slyly in the spotlights. Slyly because it is extremely difficult to know just what you *are* buying under such circumstances and it is often surprising when you unwrap your prizes at home to discover exactly what it is you have lumbered yourself with. A warning that particularly applies to paintings. It really is ill-advised to try to decipher dates, signatures and brushwork under such circumstances. But notwithstanding the inconvenience you do need to get to Bermondsey early if you want a true bargain. The gossip does not lie. Goods *do* change hands half a dozen times before noon. And there *are* sinister foreigners who whisk away selected treasures across Blackheath in vast pantechnicons before dawn has begun to streak the streets and houses with vermilion. And few questions are asked about the pedigree of the goods displayed. And much money changes hands (cash sales are the order of the day). In short, what Archer Street is to musicians and the Athenaeum to bishops, Bermondsey is to dealers.

There are some 200 open stalls in Bermondsey Square on a Friday and 120 more in the Bermondsey Antique Market (251/252 Long Lane) which is adjacent and under cover and serves hot sausage rolls.

If you fancy a stall in Bermondsey Square (and they will fancy you—I've seen new stall-holders submerge beneath the grasping hands and pitiless eyes of older dealers. It's like a Doré illustration to Dante's *Inferno*; that's the sort of welcome you'll get) you need to approach the London Borough of Southwark (01-703 6311). They will not let you have a permanent annual licence (70p) unless you have a long history of casual trading. They will suggest that you apply to the Town Clerk for a casual trader's licence (£1·20), which means that you turn up and seek out one of the two market inspectors. They will dispose of any stalls which are untenanted, although they are inclined to favour the regular applicant at the expense of the novitiate. You will need to be very patient. If your patience runs out you have a better chance of being accommodated at the Bermondsey Antique Market (01-407 4635). This will set you back £6 for the day, but at the time of writing stalls are still generally available.

The New Caledonian is not just exclusive and anti-socially early, but it is also the devil to get to without private transport. Borough

Tube is the nearest station (then walk along Long Lane) or a 42, 78, or 188 bus will take you right there. You'll be glad you made the effort. It's a surreal experience.

Camden Passage

Where the Portobello Road is an Ealing Studios Comedy, all bad puns and character actors being loveable, and Bermondsey Market is a Graham Greene film interpreted by Humphrey Bogart and Peter Lorre, Camden Passage is a Francis Durbridge serial in which everyone drinks Bacardis, the men's voices are an octave below what's natural, and The Woman blows cigarette smoke at the light fittings.

And yet the place has a respectable provenance. Since the mid-eighteenth century it has had a continuous history of small traders. Its heyday was in Victoria's reign when the Agricultural Hall was built, when the sciences were our friends and the arts part of our heritage. Between the wars it contained a coterie of little shops but it was blitzed and would not have recovered its glory had it not been for the remarkable John Friend (to whom I am indebted for this uncharacteristic scholarship). He and his wife, who was born in the Passage (don't misunderstand me!) and a group of colleagues patched up the place in the fifties, painted the shop-fronts, cemented up the bomb sites, and in short put a brave face on things. They needed to. For the first six Saturdays after Camden Passage reopened the weather was diabolical, but it survived, and they survived, and now with community festivals, chic restaurants, visiting royalty and tame Kennedys, Camden Passage flourishes. One of the two best pub theatres in London (The Orange Tree in Richmond is the other), The King's Head, is just along Upper Street, the best cinema in London, the Screen on the Green, is scarcely more than an establishing shot away, and property values are still high.

John Friend is to Camden Passage as Moses was to the Israelites, and now that he is in the land flowing with milk and honey, he's not going to settle for anything less. Standards are high. By its charter of operation, the market may only deal in antiques and 'ethnics'; no modern jewellery nor second-hand clothing (unless it's *very* second-hand) would be permitted; no more would leather belts nor transcendental candles, nor folk singers cheerfully warbling about the awful things that happened to the Indians and the Negroes and Scottish maidens.

The Passage is two hundred traffic-free yards and contains within its purlieus seventy shops, thirty boutiques and on market-days (Wednesday and Saturday) a further seventy stalls. Besides the main thoroughfare Camden Passage contains a number of arcades. There are twenty stalls in Pierrepont Market, twenty in the Charlton, which specialises in jewellery, ten in the Orange Box, twenty in Georgian Village, and similarly in the Athenai Arcade and the Flea Market. There are no plans to expand further; one property stands currently derelict since the developers' money ran out. But John Friend is hoping for continuing organic growth with a general upgrading in quality.

Wednesday is the day to go. The proceedings start at 7.45 am and the Portobello dealers are there in force stocking up for the week-end. On Saturdays you need not appear before 9.30 and business will be more genteel and leisurely, though prices may be up. Prices shouldn't be high, since the rent for the stalls is fixed at a modest £2·50 per diem, but my impression is that prices *are* high, and a picture dealer at Sotheby's confirmed my view, 'I saw a picture at Bermondsey about a year ago,' he said. 'At five o'clock it was £25, at six o'clock £45. It was sold a third time for £65, and the next day I saw it for sale in Camden Passage at £100!' (No doubt it ended up in Bond Street, a snip at £250!)

'Phone numbers if you require a stall: John Friend is at Phelps Cottage, 357 Upper Street (01-359 0190), the Athenai Arcade is run by Mr Stanley (01-226 5376) and the Flea Market is contactable on 01-226 8211 or 01-226 6627.

Take one of these buses: 19, 30, 38, 73, or a tube to The Angel, Islington.

2. The Lesser Cannons

Here's the rule for bargains: 'Do other men for they would do you'.
That's the true business precept.

Martin Chuzzlewit by Charles Dickens

The dedicated *çi-devant* (I don't know what it means, but have always wanted to use it in a book) bargain-hunter will of course visit this great triumvirate of markets from time to time, but he will spend as much time sniffing around the smaller and more spontaneous London street markets. And it is these markets which are still responsible for so much of the capital's gaiety. Buying fruit and vegetables in Harrods Food Hall is extremely reassuring if you happen to have a vested interest in the status quo (although I once saw a Harrods salesman in the fruit department strip off his white jacket, roll up his sleeves, and invite an impatient customer to 'come outside'), but Berwick Street Market is something else entirely, highly theatrical, endlessly entertaining, almost Neapolitan. There is probably nothing which can't be purchased at one or other of London's street markets, and, although few of them specialise in antiques, there's usually one or two bric-à-brac stalls, upon which you may find a Gutenberg Bible, a Turner watercolour, or a second-hand truss.

A word of warning though; like the floating crap game in *Guys and Dolls*, street markets tend to vanish and reappear quite frequently. The ones listed below should still be operating, but there may well be others which have opened since we went to press. They are in alphabetical order.

1. Cambridge Circus Market, WC2

   Only about three or four stalls. Tubby Isaac's ubiquitous jellied eels are there, also old records, prints, pictures and books (some of them rude, some of them comics).

2. Camden Lock

   This is a fairly recent antique market open Fridays and Saturdays. Some 60 stalls; interesting things.

3. Chapel Street, Islington

   Saturday and Sunday mornings. Like a miniature Portobello Road, with fruit and veg. and flowers mixed in with antiques.

4. Cheshire Street, E1 (used to be Vallance Road)

   Primarily second-hand goods and clothes but with some junk and antique stalls as well. This is a local market, and not intended for tourists (which is not to say that you won't be welcomed).

5. Church Street, Paddington

   Open Saturdays 8.30 am to about 4.30 pm. An agreeable market with pleasant pubs, the admirable Cockpit Theatre, and the School of Chiropody nearby (in case you overdo things!). At the Lisson Grove end of the market are a couple of courtyards with a handful of junky and antique stalls. Although Church Street is not as cheerful as it once was, Alfie's Market, now run by the exuberant Bernie Gray, has given it a certain seriousness. Prices are not too extravagant and there are intriguing shops in the neighbourhood with the emphasis on dolls, toys, models, chesterfields and old books.

6. Club Row (Sclater Street) off Bethnal Green Road, Shoreditch
Open Sunday mornings until about 1 pm. Specialises in pets, so if you don't want your heart broken, stay away.

7. Cutler Street, just off Petticoat Lane (Middlesex Street, q.v.), Whitechapel. Also incorporating Exchange Buildings Yard
Open Fridays, Saturdays and Sundays from 8 am, this market specialises in silver, coins, medals and stamps.

8. East Street Market, off Walworth Road
Half a mile of stalls open Tuesday to Saturday, but not Thursday afternoon. Mainly food and household goods, but you never know . . .

9. Electric Mile, Brixton
Ordinary shopping hours. Chiefly food, second-hand clothes and West Indian goods.

10. Farringdon Road, Clerkenwell
Open 11.30 am to 2.30 pm Monday to Friday and early Saturdays. Now only a sorry survival of past glories, when Farringdon Road was *the* place for old and second-hand books. A mere six stalls survive, and it is very draughty.

11. Hoxton Street, N1
Ordinary shopping hours. This market is mainly second-hand clothes, but Hoxton Street is renowned also for Hoxton Hall, now bravely trying to make a comeback as a music hall and certainly one of the prettiest theatres in the country.

12. Kingsland Waste Market, Kingsland Road, E8
Saturdays only. Household goods, electrical and cycle accessories, timber and so forth. Doesn't really belong in a book such as this one, but I've always fancied myself as eclectic.

13. Lambeth Walk, SE1
Sundays only. General.

14. Leadenhall Market, off Gracechurch Street, EC3
One of the most attractive London markets with the best butchers imaginable. (Try a capon for Christmas; ours was delicious until the dogs got it.) Leadenhall sells more or less anything and is open Monday to Friday 11 am to 3 pm (early closing Thursday).

15. Leather Lane
Monday to Friday, 11 am to 3 pm. A great variety of goods.

16. Petticoat Lane, Middlesex Street, Whitechapel
Sunday mornings. What more is there to say about Petticoat Lane? One stall announces: 'We are the only stall in London

licensed by Scotland Yard to sell stolen goods.' You can get most things in Petticoat Lane, but it's less for the serious antique hunter than for the philanthropist. Cheap clothing and silver plate are the staple ingredient of the stew.

17. Queens Crescent, Kentish Town, NW5
Ordinary shopping hours (early closing Thursday). Specialises in cheap clothes, new and second-hand, books, toys and damaged goods; bric-à-brac generally.

18. Royal Standard Antiques Market, Vanbrugh Park, Blackheath
Saturdays 9 am–5 pm. Although this pleasant market has temporarily closed there are plans for imminent reopening, so check before you make the trek up the New Kent Road (and watch out for the traffic cops; they are hard-faced men in this area of London, and the Tooley Street magistrates, though fatherly, are severe). The number to ring is 01-858 1533 and you should ask for George at the Royal Standard pub, in whose car-park the market is/was/will be situated. Goods are general antiques, prices are lower than the West End and on a fine Saturday afternoon it's worth combining this market with a stroll through Greenwich Park, or cream cakes at Florian's Delicatessen.

19. Salvation Army, Spa Road, Bermondsey
Open 10 am to 3.30 pm Monday to Friday and Saturday 9 am to 10 am for their special sale (01-237 1670). Said the Colonel (General?) I spoke to: 'You name it, we've got it', so you can check him out. It's certainly the place to go for cheap furniture.

20. Shepherds Bush Market, between Uxbridge Road and the Goldhawk Road. Ordinary shopping hours (early closing Thursday). A very large and very varied market with increasing emphasis on West Indian goods. Not notable for antiques, but always worth a visit. A jolly place.

21. Totters Market, between Middlesex Street and Goulston Street, Whitechapel
Sundays 7 am–4 pm but essential to arrive early. Really an offshoot of Petticoat Lane, this is where the rag-and-bone men bring their junk for disposal.

22. Walthamstow High Street E17
Ordinary shopping hours. Over a mile of stalls on an elegantly wide pavement; just about everything can be obtained. Crowded and noisy.

Other markets which deserve further investigation include:
  Ridley Road, E1
  Dalston Lane, E1
  Seaton Place, off Hampstead Road
  Beresford Square, Woolwich
  Tochbrook Street, Pimlico
  Swiss Cottage Market

Five: Guide to Markets throughout Britain

This guide is not all-embracing, but is intended to be representative of all types of markets where miscellaneous goods are sold, including, of course, junk and antiques. This information was collated from answers to a questionnaire. The original questions (to which the numbered answers correspond) are as follows:

1. Name and address
2. Some idea of the range of goods sold there
3. Approximately how many stalls?
4. Can anyone take a stall?
5. What is the charge, or rent?
6. To whom should one apply?
7. What day or days of the week does the market operate, and what hours?
8. Any further details

Aberdeen
Aberdeen Market, Market Street, Aberdeen (covered) 2. Miscellaneous 3. Approx. 91 4. Yes 5. Not known 6. Richard Ellis, Trafalgar House, 75 Hope Street, Glasgow G2 6AJ (041–2216196) 7. Mondays to Saturdays 8.30 a.m.–6 p.m. 8. Individual units (not stalls).

Market Stance, The Green, Aberdeen (street) 2. Fruit, flowers, vegetables, confectionary 3. 37 units for letting 4. Yes 5. 25p per day 6. Market Officer, Rates Section, City Chamberlain's Department, Town House, Aberdeen 7. Fridays and Saturdays 8 a.m.–6 p.m. 8. Very old established.

Bath

Provision Market, High Street, Bath BA1 4AW   2. General including china, glass and silverware   3. 58   4. City Council will let to approved applicants   5. £50–£100 per annum, excluding rates   6. The Director of Estate Management, North Parade Buildings, Bath BA1 INY, Bath 28411, ext. 392   7. Shopping days (early closing Thursdays).

Birkenhead

Between Market Street, Hamilton Street and Albion Street, Birkenhead   2. General   3. 175 (covered), 60 (open)   4. Yes, but register and allocation system   5. 3p per square foot per day   6. Market Superintendent, Birkenhead Market, 051–647–700, ext. 447   7. Wednesdays, Fridays and Saturdays   8. Will move in 1977 from old fire-damaged site to Grange Precinct redevelopment area.

Birmingham

Bull Ring Open Market   2. Wide range of goods and commodities   3. 150   4. Yes   5. Varies according to day   6. General Manager, Markets Department, Wolverley House, 18 Digbeth, Birmingham B5 6BJ, or market supervisor   7. Mondays to Fridays 10 a.m.–5.30 p.m.

St Martin's Retail (Rag) Market   2. Wide range of goods and commodities   3. 550   4. Yes   5. Varies according to day   6. General Manager, Markets Department, Wolverley House, 18 Digbeth, Birmingham B5 6BJ, or market supervisor   7. Mondays to Fridays 10 a.m.–5.30 p.m., Saturdays 10 a.m.–6 p.m.

Bull Ring Centre Market Hall   2. Wide range of goods and commodities   3. 197   4. Only a tenancy for a number of years   5. For assessment or sale if approved purchaser   6. The General Manager, Markets Department, Wolverley House, 18 Digbeth, Birmingham B5 6BJ, Tel: 021–622–3452   7. Mondays, Tuesdays, Thursdays, Fridays 10 a.m.–5.30 p.m.; Wednesdays 9 a.m.–1 p.m.; Saturdays 10 a.m.–6 p.m.   8. covered market.

N.B. There are also several subsidiary markets in Birmingham. Details from the Markets Department.

Bradford

John Street (covered), Bradford   2. Miscellaneous goods   3. 180   4. Controlled by the Chief Estates Officer, Estates Division, Jacob's Well, Bradford BD1 5RW   5. Various different charges   6. Correspondence to Chief Estates Officer; telephone Bradford 23876   7. Mondays to Saturdays inclusive—half day closing on Wednesdays.

Kirkgate (covered), Bradford   2. Miscellaneous goods, limited food stalls   3. 184   4. Controlled by the Chief Estates Officer, Estates Division, Jacob's Well, Bradford BD1 5RW   5. Various different charges   6. Correspondence to Chief Estates Officer; telephone Bradford 23876   7. Mondays to Saturdays inclusive—half-day closing on Wednesdays.

Market Hall, Keighley (covered), Bradford   2. Miscellaneous goods   3. 82   4. Controlled by the Chief Estates Officer, Estates Division, Jacob's

Well, Bradford BD1 5RW   5. Various different charges   6. Correspondence to Chief Estates Officer; telephone Bradford 23876   7. Mondays to Saturdays inclusive—half-day closing Tuesdays.

Market Hall, Shipley (covered), Bradford   2. Miscellaneous goods   3. 42   4. Controlled by the Chief Estates Officer, Estates Division, Jacob's Well, Bradford BD1 5RW   5. Various different charges are made for these markets   6. Correspondence to Chief Estates Officer; telephone Bradford 23876   7. Mondays to Saturdays inclusive—half-day closing on Wednesdays.

Open Market, Shipley, Bradford   2. Miscellaneous goods   3. 47   4. Controlled by the Chief Estates Officer, Estates Division, Jacob's Well, Bradford BD1 5RW   5. £2 per stall per day   6. Correspondence to Chief Estates Officer; telephone Bradford 23876   7. Fridays and Saturdays.

Open Market, Bingley, Bradford   2. Miscellaneous   3. 13   4. Controlled by the Chief Estates Officer, Estates Division, Jacob's Well, Bradford BD1 5RW   5. £2 per stall per day   6. Correspondence to Chief Estates Officer; telephone Bradford 23876   7. Tuesdays and Saturdays

Brighton
The Open Market, London Road, Brighton, Sussex   2. General   3. 42   4. Stalls let on lease. Assignments permitted in certain cases, but rarely does a stall become vacant for letting by the Council   5. See (4)   6. Borough Estates Surveyor, 26/30 Kings Road, Brighton BN1 1PE; telephone Brighton (0273) 29801, ext. 655   7. Mondays 7 a.m.–1 p.m., Tuesdays–Thursdays 7 a.m.–5 p.m., Fridays and Saturdays 7 a.m.–6 p.m.

Upper Gardner Street, Brighton, Sussex   2. Bric-à-brac, antiques, junk   3. 92   4. Yes, if private individuals, not firms or organisations; long waiting list   5. £11 per annum plus 50p deposit for arm badge   6. Borough Secretary, Town Hall, Brighton, Sussex 0273–29801, ext. 481   7. Saturday mornings   8. Traders provide own stalls; thriving street market, spilling over into adjoining privately owned sites.

Bristol
St Nicholas Miscellaneous Market   2. Miscellaneous   3. 50   4. Yes, but preference given to local residents   5. £2 per square foot, per annum, payable monthly in advance   6. The Markets Superintendent, The Exchange, Corn Street, Bristol BS1 1JQ·   7. Mondays to Saturdays 30 hours per week.

Exchange Hall   2. Antiques and Collector's Market   6. As above   7. Every Friday.

Cambridge
Cambridge City Council Street Market, Market Hill, Cambridge   2. Miscellaneous, including books and antiques   3. 103   4. Yes   5. 85p–£2·10 per day   6. City Engineer and Surveyor's Department, The Guildhall, Cambridge (telephone 58977)   7. Mondays–Saturdays 7 a.m.–5 p.m.   8. Just as it was at the beginning of the century.

Canterbury

Herne Bay General Market, Beach Street, Herne Bay   2. General Merchandise   3. 240   4. Yes   5. £2·25 per stall   6. E. J. Lea, Market Agent, 163 High Street, Milton Regis, Sittingbourne, Kent   7. Saturdays 8 a.m.–4 p.m.

Carlisle

Covered Market, Scotch Street, Carlisle   2. Everything   3. 60+   4. Yes, waiting list, let on monthly basis   5. £3 for 6ft frontage per day, more for larger stall   6. Mrs M. McBride, Markets Manager, Scotch Street, Carlisle, Cumbria (telephone 22232)   7. Daily except Thursday (closes at 1 p.m.) Mondays to Wednesdays 7.30 a.m.–5.30 p.m., Fridays and Saturdays 7.30 a.m.–6 p.m.   8. Fridays and Saturdays busiest; no casuals or 'pitching'.

Cleveland

Racecourse, West Dyke Road, Redcar   2. General   3. 30   4. Only those permitted to trade on Sundays   5. Not known   6. Mr T. Anderson, Stork Hotel, Bowesfield Lane, Stockton-on-Tees, Cleveland (Stockton 611939)   7. Sundays 10 a.m.–2 p.m.

South Bank, Langbaurgh, Cleveland   2. General   3. 60   4. Subject to registration and vacancies, casuals who attend regularly given preference   5. 40p stallage, 50p + VAT stall hire (increase being considered)   6. Chief Environmental Health Officer, Municipal Buildings, Coatham Road, Redcar, Cleveland (Redcar 73121)   7. Fridays 9 a.m.–4.30 p.m.

Westgate, Guisborough, Cleveland   2. General   3. 20   4. Not known   5. Not known   6. Lord Guisborough's Land Agent, A. W. Watts & Co, 26 Harewood Lane, Romanby, Northallerton (Northallerton 2793)   7. Thursdays and Saturdays.

Coventry

City of Coventry Retail Market, Queen Victoria Road, Coventry   2. Miscellaneous   3. 229   4. Yes   5. £15·18 per week inclusive   6. General Manager, Markets Department, The Public Abattoir, Upper York Street, Coventry (telephone 22254).

Deal

Car Park, High Street, Deal (open)   2. All trades   3. 9   4. Yes, providing there are vacancies   5. £1 ratepayers, £2 non-ratepayers   6. Mr A. D. Cowie, The Town Sergeant, Town Hall, Deal, Kent (Deal 4963)   7. Saturdays 8 a.m.–6 p.m.

Sandwich Cattle Market (open)   2. All trades   3. 35 stalls, 18 pitches   4. Yes, providing there are vacancies   5. £1·30 stalls, 90p pitches   6. The Chief Valuer, New Bridge House, New Bridge, Dover, Kent (Dover 206090)   7. Thursdays 8 a.m.–3 p.m.   8. As large a variety as possible.

Derby

Morledge Market, Derby DE1 2AZ 2. Miscellaneous 3. 319 4. Yes, except persons holding full-time employment or Ltd. Companies 5. £25–£32 per week 6. W. J. Shaw, Markets Officer, Conal House, Derby (Derby 31111, ext. 694) 7. Tuesdays, Thursdays, Fridays, Saturdays 8 a.m.–6 p.m.

Market Hall 2. Miscellaneous 3. 154 4. Yes, except Ltd. Companies 5. New tenants on tendered rent system 6. W. J. Shaw, Markets Officer, Conal House, Derby (Derby 31111, ext. 694) 7. 5½ days, 8 a.m.–5.30 p.m. (Wednesdays early closing).

Allenton Market 2. Miscellaneous 3. 90 4. Yes, except persons holding full-time employment or Ltd. Companies 5. £1·15–£1·40 per day 6. W. J. Shaw, Markets Officer, Conal House, Derby (Derby 31111, ext. 694) 7. Fridays and Saturdays 8 a.m.–6 p.m.

Edinburgh

Ingleston, Edinburgh 2. Everything, 'even insurance policies' 3. 1200 (maximum) 4. Yes 5. £3·50 for covered stall 13' × 5' 6. Spook Erection, Moreton-in-the-Marsh, Glos. GL56 OAD 7. Sundays 10 a.m.–4 p.m. 8. Claimed to be largest in world. Peaks in summertime.

Exeter

Covered Market, New Lower Market, Fore Street, Exeter 2. General 3. 44 stalls; 25 kiosk shops; 4 shops in market entrance 4. Yes, subject to availability (no old clothes!) 5. 12p–29p per foot depending on day and size 6. W. D. Johnson, Markets Superintendent, Markets Office, 23 New Cattle Market, Marsh Barton Road, Exeter (telephone Exeter 56847).

Cattle Market, Marsh Barton Road, Exeter 2. General 3. 120 maximum 4. Yes 5. £3 per 7ft stall 6. Mr. W. Hacker, 'Lindridge', 41 Edward Road, Clevedon BS21 7DT Avon (telephone Clevedon 4517) 8. New venture.

Great Yarmouth

Great Yarmouth Corporation Open Market 2. Miscellaneous 3. Wednesdays 125, Saturdays 139 4. No casuals, only accepted if stall licensed for same commodity, and is vacant 5. £1·10 for 8' site, plus £1·62 per diem stall hire, plus VAT 6. Estates Surveyor and Valuer, Municipal Buildings, Hall Plain, Gt. Yarmouth NR30 2QG (telephone 0493-3233/3283) 7. Saturdays and Wednesdays 7.30–5.30 8. May–September busy, winter quiet.

Guildford

Guildford Cattle Market, General Trading Market, Slyfield Green, Guildford 2. Car auctions and general 3. 200 stalls 4. Yes, subject to lessors' approval 5. Charge determined by principal lessors 6. Messrs Weller Eggar and Co, Auctioneers, Cattle Market, Slyfield Green, Guildford GU1 1RL (telephone 73386) 7. Wednesdays and on certain public holidays.

Guildford Society Draft Market, Tunsgate Arch (east side), Guildford 2. Local crafts 3. 5 4. For determination by Guildford Society 5. £5 per day 6. The Guildford Society, Mr J. Tatlon, 14a The Mount, Guildford 7. Specific Saturdays in December after 10.00 a.m. as agreed by the Council, and in mid-summer.

Hartlepool

Market Hall, Middleton Grange Shopping Centre, Hartlepool (covered) 2. Fruit and vegetables, household goods, carpets, crockery, clothing, toys, handbags, sweets, cakes, bread, etc. 3. 19 4. Apply to Council 5. Small stall £876 per annum, big stall £1,748 per annum 6. Hartlepool Borough Council, Borough Treasurer's Department, Avenue Road, Hartlepool (telephone 4112) 7. All week except Wednesday afternoons 8. In modern shopping centre.

Avenue Road, South Road, Hartlepool (open) 2. As above, plus radios, dress materials, books, refreshments 3. 64 4. Apply to Director of Leisure and Amenities, Hartlepool 5. £3 per diem 6. Hartlepool Borough Council, Director of Leisure and Amenities, Municipal Buildings, Hartlepool (telephone 72161) 7. Thursdays 10 a.m.–4 p.m. 8. Adjacent to modern shopping centre.

Inverness

Town Centre, Inverness 2. General 3. Approx. 13 shops and 18 stalls 4. Apply to Council 5. Variable 6. Chief Executive, Inverness District Council, Town House, Inverness (telephone Inverness 39111) 7. Mondays to Saturdays 9 a.m.–5.30 p.m.

Vacant site of former Playhouse Cinema, also Town Centre (open) 2. General, including bric-à-brac 3. Approx. 18 stalls 4. Not known 5. Not known 6. Secretary, Caledonian Associated Cinemas Ltd., 4 Academy Street, Inverness (telephone 37611) 7. Saturdays only 10 a.m.–4 p.m.

Leeds

Market Hall, Seacroft Town Centre, Leeds 14 2. Miscellaneous 3. 67 4. Yes 5. £1 per stall per diem, to be increased to £1·50 6. Director of Estates and Development, Centre Management Office, 294 North Parkway, Leeds 14 7. Fridays and Saturdays 9 a.m.–6 p.m.

Kirkgate General Market, Vicar Lane, Leeds 2 2. Miscellaneous 3. 116 4. Yes 5. £11–£55 per week according to size 6. Market Manager, Leeds City Council, 12 Market Buildings, Vicar Lane. Leeds 2 (456245) 7. Mondays to Saturdays 7 a.m.–6 p.m. (early closing Wednesdays).

Kirkgate Open Market, Leeds 2 2. Miscellaneous 3. Approx. 130 4. Yes 5. £4 per diem, £2 half stall, £1 quarter stall 6. As above 7. Tuesdays, Fridays, Saturdays 8 a.m.–6 p.m.

Leicester
Open Market, Market Place, Leicester   2. General, including antiques   3.
321   4. Let by trader   5. Basic charges from £1·50–£9 according to size,
position and day   6. Market Manager, City Estates Department, Alliance
House, Bishop Street, Leicester (Leicester 58862); casuals by 9 a.m. on day
in question to Toll Collector's office, Market Centre   7. Tuesdays to
Saturdays

Market Centre, Market Place, Leicester (covered)   2. General, including
antiques   3. 78 and 11 shops and kiosks   4. Yes   5. Let by trader, basic
charges £1·50–£9 according to size and position   6. Market Manager, City
Estates Department, Alliance House, Bishop Street, Leicester (Leicester
58862); casuals by 9 a.m. on day in question to Toll Collector's office,
Market Centre   7. Mondays to Saturdays   8. Individual market trading
'but some degree of "store" atmosphere and advantages'.

Liverpool
North General Market, Great Homer Street, Liverpool L5 3LQ; tel: 207
0601   2. New and secondhand clothing and goods   3. 170   4. Waiting
list, but spaces allocated for the day if non-attendance of traders with
reservations   5. £1·10 per diem   6. The Inspector, St Martin's Market,
Great Homer Street, Liverpool L5 3LQ   7. Saturdays 9 a.m.–5 p.m.   8.
Secondhand goods restricted to one area of market; uncovered; adjoins St
Martin's Market.

St Martin's Market, Great Homer Street, Liverpool L5 3LQ   2. New and
secondhand clothing and goods   3. 116   4. Waiting list, vacancies offered
in date order of application   5. £4·10 per week   6. The Inspector, St
Martin's Market; tel: 207–0601   7. Mondays to Saturdays 9 a.m.–5 p.m.,
but Wednesdays 9 a.m.–1 p.m.

Garston Market, Island Road South, Garston, Liverpool   2. New and
secondhand clothing and goods   3. 163   4. Waiting list of casual applicants   5. £1·45   6. The Inspector, Garston Market   7. Tuesdays and
Fridays 8 a.m.–6 p.m.

Maidstone
Lockmeadow Market, Maidstone   2. Anything saleable   3. 500   4.
Yes   5. From   £1·50   6. Market   Manager,   Manager's   Office,
Lockmeadow Market, Barker Road, Maidstone, Kent (Maidstone 671361,
ext. 171)   7. Tuesdays, approximately 7 a.m.–2 p.m.   8. True atmosphere
of a county town market.

Manchester
Retail Market, Grey Mare Lane, Bradford, Manchester 11   2. Miscellan-
eous   3. 97 stalls, 30 stands   4. Yes   5. £7–£9 per week   6. Director of
Markets, Cumberland House, Crown Square, Manchester M60 3BB   7.
Mondays, Wednesdays, Fridays and Saturdays.

Longsight Retail Market, Dickenson Road, Longsight, Manchester 13   2.
Miscellaneous   3. 104 stalls, 15 food stalls, 27 stands   4. Yes   5. £8–£14
per week   6. As above   7. Wednesdays, Fridays and Saturdays.

Moss Side Retail Market, Denhill Street, Moss Side, Manchester 16   2. Miscellaneous   3. 66 stalls, 8 shops   4. Yes   5. Stalls £20–£30 per week, shops £1,200 per annum plus rates and service charge   6. As above   7. Mondays to Saturdays (except Wednesdays).

Wythenshawe Retail Market, Rowlands Way, Civic Centre, Wythenshawe, Manchester 22   2. Miscellaneous   3. 136 general, 28 food stalls and 14 fruit and vegetable   4. Yes   5. General £8·30–£8·90 per week   6. As above   7. Open market Tuesdays, Fridays and Saturdays.

Gorton Retail Market, Gortoncross Street, Gorton, Manchester 18   2. Miscellaneous   3. 96 general, 20 food (including café), 9 fruit and vegetable, 9 shops   4. Yes   5. General £8·30–£8·90 per week, shops £1,250–£2,000 per annum   6. As above   7. Open section Tuesdays, Fridays, Saturdays.

Harpurhey Retail Market, Rochdale Road, Harpurhey, Manchester 9   2. Miscellaneous   3. 128 general, 28 food (including café), 12 fruit and vegetable   4. Yes   5. General £8·30–£8·90 per week   6. As above   8. Open section opened April 1976.

Central Retail Market, High Street, Manchester 1   2. Miscellaneous   3. 193 stalls, 15 shops in covered market   4. Yes   5. To be determined   6. As above   7. To be determined.

Middlesbrough
North Ormesby Market, Kings Road, North Ormesby, Middlesbrough   2. Miscellaneous   3. 152   4. Yes, subject to availability. Casual list from which vacancies are filled   5. £3·18 for 10′ × 7′ stall, standage only £1·05   6. Chief Environmental Health Office, Environmental Health Officer, Marton House, Borough Road, Middlesbrough, Cleveland TS4 2EH (0642 45432 ext. 3924/5)   7. Tuesdays and Saturdays 9 a.m.–7 p.m.

Newcastle-upon-Tyne
Grainger Market, Grainger Street, Newcastle-upon-Tyne (covered)   2. Extensive, including antiques   3. 135   4. Yes, providing overall tenant/trade balance is retained   5. Not known   6. L. Humphries, City Estate and Property Surveyor, Civic Centre, Newcastle-upon-Tyne (telephone 28520)   7. Mondays 8 a.m.–5 p.m., Tuesdays, Thursdays, Saturdays 8 a.m.–5.30 p.m., Wednesdays 8 a.m.–1 p.m., Fridays 8 a.m.–6 p.m.   8. Opened 1835, Grade II listed building; 'chaste and classic elegance'.

Bigg Market (street)   2. Miscellaneous   3. 30   4. Pitches allocated according to waiting list   5. Not known   6. L. Humphries, City Estate and Property Surveyor, Civic Centre, Newcastle-upon-Tyne (28520)   7. Tuesdays, Thursdays, Saturdays 9 a.m.–5 p.m.   8. Name derives from 'bigg'— a kind of barley, continuing tradition of markets on site; now much smaller than it was.

Norwich
Norwich City Council Provision Market—in the square in front of City Hall, Norwich   2. General   3. 202   4. Yes, providing one is available   5.

Weekly £5·25–£9·60, daily Mondays to Fridays £1·05–£1·30, Saturdays £2·00–£2·30   6. Norwich City Council, Markets Division, 13 Red Lion Street, Norwich (Norwich 22233)   7. Mondays to Saturdays   8. Popular with holiday makers. Being modernised with new stalls.

Nottingham
Victoria Market, Victoria Shopping Centre   2. Miscellaneous   3. 138 (lower floor), 28 (upper level)   4. Yes—lower floor let on tenancies, upper level on daily lettings   5. Lower floor assessed; upper level 12½p per foot frontage (Mondays, Tuesdays, Wednesdays), 10p (Thursdays), 15p (Fridays and Saturdays)   6. Markets and Fairs Division, Victoria Market, Nottingham, or see Market Superintendent 9.30–10.00 a.m.   7. Mondays to Saturdays   8. Large modern market.

Bulwell Market, Bulwell, Nr. Nottingham   2. Wide range of general merchandise   3. 45   4. Yes   5. £2·25 per diem   6. Markets and Fairs Division, Victoria Market, Nottingham, or see the Superintendent 9.30–10.00 a.m.   7. Tuesdays, Fridays and Saturdays, 10.00 a.m.–5.00 p.m.   8. Open market

Sneinton Retail Market, Bath Street, Nottingham   2. Great variety of goods   3. 110 ground spaces   4. Yes   5. 15p per foot frontage per diem   6. Markets and Fairs Division, Victoria Market, Nottingham, or see the Superintendent, 9.30–10.00 a.m.   7. Mondays and Saturdays, 9.00 a.m.–1.00 p.m.   8. Entertainment by pitchers and demonstrators, very crowded.

Penzance
Causewayhead, Penzance   2. Miscellaneous   3. Between 4 and 8   4. Yes   5. Between £2·50 and £5·00 per day   6. The Market Superintendent, Council Offices, St Clare, Penzance   7. Tuesdays, Thursdays and Saturdays 9.00 a.m.–5.30 p.m.

Plymouth
Central Market, New George Street, Plymouth   2. Miscellaneous   3. 144 permanent, 16 fish, 6 cakes, 64 'daily benches'   4. Benches to anyone, subject to suitability of trade and availability of accommodation; other stalls permanently occupied   5. 48p–£1·21 per day depending on location and day   6. Market Superintendent, Central Market, New George Street, Plymouth (68000)   7. Mondays, Tuesdays, Thursdays and Saturdays 8 a.m.–5.30 p.m., Wednesdays 8 a.m.–1 p.m., Fridays 8 a.m.–6 p.m.   8. Part of rebuilt centre of Plymouth.

Portsmouth
Charlotte Street, Moores Square, Portsmouth   2. Food and household   3. 30–40   4. Yes, as available   5. £7 for three days and £3·50 for each additional day in Charlotte Street; £9 for three days and £4·50 for each additional day in Moores Square   6. The Market Inspector, The Tricorn, Portsmouth (Portsmouth 27354)   7. Thursdays, Fridays, Saturdays   8. Over 100 years standing; narrow bustling street and small square.

74

The Tricorn Market, The Tricorn, Portsmouth (adjacent to above) 2. Shoes, clothes, jewellery, Indian goods, etc. 3. Not known 4. Yes 5. Not known 6. Africa House, 64/78 Kingsway London WC2 7. Thursdays, Fridays, Saturdays.

Preston

Earl Street/Lancaster Road, Preston 2. Miscellaneous, including antiques 3. 120 4. Yes 5. From £1·20 to £3·00 depending on day and cover 6. The Markets Superintendent, Earl Street, Preston (57213) 7. Mondays, Wednesdays, Fridays and Saturdays 7.30 a.m.–6 p.m. 8. Open market with traditional atmosphere.

Earl Street/Market Street, Preston 2. Miscellaneous, including antiques 3. 36 4. Yes 5. From £1·20 to £3·00 depending on day and cover 6. The Markets Superintendent, Earl Street, Preston (57213) 7. Mondays, Wednesdays, Fridays and Saturdays 7.30 a.m.–6 p.m. 8. Open market with traditional atmosphere.

Sheffield

Castle Market, Exchange Street, Sheffield 2. Miscellaneous 3. 240 4. Lettings by tender as available 5. Not known 6. Markets and Abattoir Superintendent, 5th Floor, Castle Market Building, Exchange Street, Sheffield (135280) 7. Mondays, Tuesdays, Wednesdays 8 a.m.–5 p.m., Fridays 8 a.m.–6 p.m., Saturdays 8 a.m.–5.30 p.m.

Sheaf Market, Exchange Street, Sheffield, 2. Miscellaneous 3. 283 4. Lettings by tender as available 5. Not known 6. Markets and Abattoir Superintendent, 5th Floor, Castle Market Building, Exchange Street, Sheffield (135280) 7. Mondays, Tuesdays, Wednesdays 9 a.m.–5 p.m., Fridays 9 a.m.–6 p.m., Saturdays 9 a.m.–5.30 p.m.

The Setts Market, Exchange Street, Sheffield 2. Miscellaneous 3. 45 4. Let from casual traders' attendance register 5. Not known 6. Markets and Abattoir Superintendent, 5th Floor, Castle Market Building, Exchange Street, Sheffield (135280) 7. Tuesdays 8 a.m.–5 p.m., Fridays 8 a.m.–6 p.m., Saturdays 8 a.m.–5.30 p.m.

The Moorfoot Market, The Moor, Sheffield 2. Miscellaneous 3. 36 4. Let by tender 5. Not known 6. Markets and Abattoir Superintendent, 5th Floor, Castle Market Building, Exchange Street, Sheffield (135280) 7. Tuesdays 8 a.m.–5.30 p.m., Fridays 8 a.m.–6 p.m., Saturdays 8 a.m.–5.30 p.m.

Stocksbridge Market, Manchester Road, Stocksbridge, Sheffield 2. Miscellaneous 3. 35 4. Let from mailing list 5. Not known 6. Markets and Abattoir Superintendent, 5th Floor, Castle Market Building, Exchange Street, Sheffield (135280) 7. Fridays 8 a.m.–6 p.m.

Southampton

Kingsland Market, St Mary Street, Southampton 2. Miscellaneous 3. 60 stalls 4. Waiting list 5. £7·50 per week 6. Director of Housing, Civic Centre, Southampton SO9 4XR (23855, ext. 231) 7. Mondays to

Saturdays 7 a.m.–7 p.m. (Thursdays to Saturdays busiest) 8. For other, private markets, contact Southampton Trades Council, 3 Cheddar Close, Woolston, Southampton.

Stoke-on-Trent

Tunstall, High Street, Tunstall, Stoke-on-Trent (84656); Burslem, Queen Street, Burslem, Stoke-on-Trent (84791); Hanley General, Market Square, Hanley, Stoke-on-Trent (22561); Stoke, Church Street, Stoke-on-Trent (45874); Longton, Time Square, Longton 2. Miscellaneous 3. 349 in six markets (covered) 4. Yes, but not Limited Companies, waiting list 5. £5–£25 depending on frontage area and which market 6. City Estates Management Officer, Victoria Chambers, Church Street, Stoke-on-Trent ST4 1DL (48241, ext. 463) 7. Wednesdays, Fridays and Saturdays 8.30 a.m.–5.30 p.m.

Open market at Burslem (30 stalls owned by City Council) let on same basis as covered markets, open on Saturdays from 9 a.m. to 5.30 p.m. for which a toll of £3 is paid.

Open Market in Hanley Market Square on Wednesdays, Fridays and Saturdays—4 miscellaneous stalls, 6 market garden stalls.

Swansea

Swansea Market, Oxford Street, Swansea 2. Foodstuffs, hardware 3. Approximately 700, largest in Wales 4. Yes 5. Variable, dependent on site, size, etc. 6. City Estate Agent, The Guildhall, Swansea (0792 50821) 7. Shopping hours (Thursdays early closing) 8. Much local produce, including cockles, laverbread, *bara gwyedd*, Welsh cakes, etc.

Thanet

Dumpton Market, Dumpton Greyhound Stadium, Ramsgate, Kent (open) 2. Anything and everything (almost) 3. Maximum of 306 4. Yes, but not so easy in summer 5. Approximately £2·50 per day 6. Mr Lea (manager), Dumpton Market, Dumpton Greyhound Stadium, Ramsgate, Kent (Thanet 53333) 7. Fridays only, 8 a.m.–4 p.m.

East Ham Shopping Hall Ltd., 38 Harbour Street, Ramsgate, Kent (covered) 2. Anything and everything 3. 6 4. Not known 5. Not known 6. The Manager, 33 Market Place, Romford, Essex RM1 3AB (telephone 40492) 7. Mondays to Saturdays, normal shopping hours.

Dreamland Market, Dreamland Amusement Market, Margate, Kent 2. Anything and everything 3. 50 4. Not known 5. Not known 6. The Manager, Dreamland Estates Ltd, Dreamland, Margate, Kent (Thanet 21212) 7. Fridays—mornings only.

Truro

Premier Market, Lemon Quay, Truro 2. General 3. 40–45 4. Yes 5. Not known 6. Mr Tyson, Miller & Co., Estate Agents, Mansion House, Prince Street, Truro (telephone 4211) 7. Wednesdays, Fridays and Saturdays 9 a.m.–5 p.m. 8. Car Park opposite

Creation Centre, Back Quay, Truro 2. Everything, with a special emphasis on Cornish crafts 3. Approx. 50 4. No 5. Not known 6. Mr Fox, Creation Centre, Back Quay, Truro (telephone 3486) 7. Wednesdays, Fridays and Saturdays 9 a.m.–5.30 p.m.

Wolverhampton
Central Market Hall and open market, School Street, Wolverhampton 2. Miscellaneous 3. Central—126 stalls and shops, open—145 stalls and tables 4. Covered, let by tender; open, let on basis of licences but unoccupied stalls are available for casual traders 5. Stall £4 per diem; table £3 per diem 6. General Manager, City Markets, Wolverhampton (telephone 21571) 7. Tuesdays, Wednesdays, Fridays, Saturdays 8 a.m.–5 p.m.

Bilston Market Hall and Open Market, Market Street, Bilston, Wolverhampton 2. Miscellaneous 3. Bilston 88 stalls, open 130 tables 4. Covered, let by tender; open, let on basis of licences, but unoccupied stalls are available for casual traders 5. Stalls £3·50–£4·25 per diem 6. Mr F. Wylde, Supervisor, Bilston, Wolverhampton (telephone 43816) 7. Mondays, Fridays, Saturdays 8 a.m.–6 p.m.

Wednesfield Open Market, Alfred Squire Road, Wednesfield, Wolverhampton 2. Miscellaneous 3. 72 shops and stalls 4. Let on basis of licences, but unoccupied stalls available to casual traders 5. £1·42 per diem 6. Mr V. Hatton, Supervisor, Wednesfield, Wolverhampton (telephone 737145) 7. Tuesdays, Fridays, Saturdays 8 a.m.–6 p.m.

York
Newgate Market, York 2. General 3. 122 4. Yes, York applicants have priority 5. £1–£2 6. The Market Superintendent, Market and Fairs Department, 2 Newgate, York 7. Tuesdays–Saturdays 7.30 a.m.–5.30 p.m.

PART 2

What to buy

People who like this sort of thing will find this the sort of thing they like.

Abraham Lincoln

So now you know where to go for your bargains and how to outwit the fifty million others in the field, all that remains is to decide what to buy. Being pig-ignorant when I started as a junkard I formulated certain rules which have proved convenient and workable, and which have kept the bailiff away from our door. And, though I have no stone tablets, I am happy to pass these rules on to you for what they're worth.

1. *I never pay much for anything.* This maybe is innate meanness as much as deliberate policy, but it has proved to be sound policy nonetheless. Twenty-five pounds is about my limit and within that limit I have found (and kept): an eighteenth-century glass engraving in a maplewood frame (£22); an old Knowle settee upholstered in brocade (£15); an old oak linen chest (£8); an inlaid mahogany open bookcase (£13); Victorian floral decorated tiles for our fireplace (a complete set for £13); a bergère armchair with cane back, tapestry upholstery, and carved panels (£2); a Victorian bead footstool (£7); a huge old stoneware salter, in which we keep the dogfood because the puppy can't yet open it (£3·50); an engaging leafy wrought-iron gas bracket converted to electricity (£2), and many other agreeable artefacts.

Yvonne collects small china animals marked with town crests; our limit for these is £2·50, and our limit for the much more attractive miniature jugs is £1·25. We seldom pack up after an antique fair without one animal or jug to add to our collection. We also collect odd plates and coffee cups—so much less upsetting when you drop one, and so much cheaper than buying sets.

I mention these autobiographical details not from boastfulness—though there is pleasure to be got out of boasting if you can find impressionable house guests—but as proof that even in the inflationary seventies bargains are there for the asking.

Of course there have been disasters, too. The fake Staffordshire, the reproduction Sunderland lustreware (reproduction *and* cracked!), the brewer's hydrometer, and 'antique miniature chest' (those wretched catalogues!), the chairs that fell to pieces, the shoulder-bag full of pennies (I couldn't resist them but what do you *do* with over £10 worth of withdrawn currency?), those 'nostalgic gramophones, made under licence from EMI in Spain' and both quite useless, and so on. Yet the rule is sound. If you don't pay much, you can't lose much.

2. This follows on from Rule 1. *I will cut my losses.* If I realise I've blundered (again!) I will cheerfully sell the items at a loss or put them into another auction directly, in the hopes that another fool will fall into the pit. The trouble arises when I don't realise that I've blundered. Pride cometh after a ᶠall, and it is pride which causes me sometimes to continue to flog the poor old horse long after it is well and truly dead. But then there's always Rule 3.

3. *I won't worry.* The logic is that disasters are inevitable, and that the only true disaster is *making the same mistake twice.* I try very hard not to do this.

But where I was pig-ignorant, I know that I am now no better than piglet-ignorant. There will come a time when I have a little knowledge (which is dangerous but only when mixing with those who have more), and then one day I shall know it all and die rich and hated and surrounded by precious things, all genuine and all bought amazingly cheap. Since it will then be too late to pass on my knowledge (except maybe at Spiritualist meetings) I pass on a few hints, which have proved helpful at least to me. They are alphabetically arranged.

I include up-to-date prices from sales which I have attended and price lists which auctioneers have sent me, and a recommended book or books on each subject, which will offer more detailed and specialised information, should you need it. All books named are in print.

Books

The small old-fashioned book, for which you need only pay six-pence at a bookstall, works miracles to this day, turning bitter waters into sweetness.   *The Mill on the Floss*, by George Eliot

Well, of course, you *could* go out and search the second-hand bookshops for a Gutenberg Bible, and really I have no wish to be a wet blanket, but it's not to be recommended. If you like books (and George Eliot is right, the cost of buying a book is out of all proportion to the effect the book may have on your life), then the best thing to do, at least to begin with and while you're learning, is to go to country auctions and buy books in large and assorted quantities. For a pound (boasting again!) I picked up a small library of between-the-wars girls' school stories—Angela Brazils and the like. They are beautifully bound, look very nice in the bedroom and are highly erotic in a starched-apron kind of way. They were a bargain, and that is what this book is all about. Thus, at any auction of effects and house contents you are likely to be able to pick up a tea-chest full of books for between £10 and £20. You'll not know what you've got till you get them home, but you're sure to find (I promise) one or two treasures. In our last tea-chest was a delightful edition of *The Water Babies*, illustrated by W. Heath Robinson. This and a couple of hundred other volumes for the price of two modern novels—ridiculous! You may find scrap albums or stamp albums or cigarette cards, letters or diaries or recipe books; you may find absolutely anything: a great game.

The price of books being what it is, you can also pick up sets of the classics at bargain prices. I bought twenty-eight volumes of Waverley novels for a pound and sold them to my brother-in-law at a huge profit (he's a lawyer, so it didn't matter). But here, from a

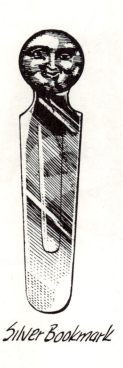

Silver Bookmark

Top-end of Woven Silk Bookmark.

1975 auction in the Isle of Wight, are a few examples of the sort of thing you can expect:

    23 volumes of Thackeray—£6

    3 volumes of *Arabian Nights' Entertainments*—£7

    12 volumes of Pepys—£12

    20 volumes of Dickens—£20

    25 volumes of the 9th edition of the *Encyclopaedia Britannica* (complete)—£12

    6 volumes of Winston Churchill's *The Second World War*—£5

But no need to rush off to the Isle of Wight. These examples are typical, although in four years prices have risen a bit.

First editions are tricky things, and may not be as valuable as you suppose (so far as my novels are concerned second editions are the collectors' items). Very old books are sometimes valuable, but not always, so it may be wisest to concentrate—if you want to concentrate and not just go tea-chesting—on leather- and calf-bound books and out-of-print books on birds, military history, wild life, medical and mechanical subjects, and so on; these tend to fetch a lot of money. F. O. Morris's fine *British Birds* in 6 volumes is worth about £100 (the price varies a little according to the edition) and similarly with other illustrated and specialist works. Nicely illustrated children's books are always in demand and fetch prices equivalent to new children's books, giving another indication of the craziness of our values and the opportunity for you to pick up a bargain. Good luck!

Books: *The Collector's Book of Books* by Eric Quaile (Studio Vista, 1971)

Book Collecting: A Beginner's Guide by Seamas Stewart (David & Charles, 1972)

Chairs

I had three chairs in my house; one for solitude, two for friendship, three for society.

Walden by H. D. Thoreau

I doubt whether any of the vital decisions of history were made sitting down. And when in *Richard II* old John of Gaunt (an agreeable part for an actor, a splendid speech, plenty of applause, and home early enough to catch *News at Ten*) announces: 'Methinks I am a prophet new inspired . . .' he traditionally rises to his shaky feet, for inspiration is not supposed to come when you are sedentary or prone. Kings were given thrones ostensibly to pander to their conceit, but in reality to stop them thinking too clearly, while their counsellors strode up and down, Having Ideas. The best Prime Ministers have not been sitters, although some (Stanley Baldwin, Harold Wilson) have used chairs—with pipes—to conjure up an image of reliability and unflappability. You may trust a man who sits, but it implies a measure of decadence and the Women's Lib movement have their priorities right when they take offence at being offered seats in public places.

The Early English seldom sat except on benches at meal-times, and occasionally stools, nor was it until the early seventeenth century that chairs caught on—and then they were huge and brutish bishops' thrones-type chairs. From then on the history of chairs (and the history of furniture) has a pleasant kind of logic to it. Throughout the eighteenth century chairs went on a diet; that is to say, whatever could be pared down was pared down and whatever could be whittled away was whittled away. Throughout the nineteenth century they grew gradually fatter once again.

Seventeenth-century chairs were made from native woods—oak, elm, walnut (especially), laburnum and fruitwoods—and it wasn't until the Palladian revival when William Kent brought Italian baroque designs to England that there was any radical change in English styles. Kent's designs were reflected in *The City and Country Workmen's Treasury* (1739) and he was one of the first to exploit, though sparingly, the possibilities of that dashing new timber, Jamaican mahogany.

Amongst other great craftsmen of this period, Thomas Chippendale (1718–1779) stands out, for it was he who reduced the heavy square legs to the cabriole style and curbed the more excessive fancies of the rococo style. His catalogue *The Gentleman and Cabinet-Maker's Directory* (1754) was extremely influential, not least with George Hepplewhite who removed the stretchers, pierced the backs, narrowed the legs and lightened the splats of the Chippendale style. Hepplewhite's most distinctive chair is the shield-back, and he also fancied serpentine fronts, Prince of Wales plumes and satinwood inlay on his favoured mahogany.

Robert Adam (1728–1792) was the prophet of neo-Classicism with honeysuckle and rams' heads and swags and urns—the same kind of symbolism which appealed to Wedgwood in china. Adam also experimented with filigree carving, and Thomas Sheraton (1751–1806), who produced his important *Cabinet Makers' and Upholsterers' Drawing Book* at the end of the eighteenth century, encouraged even lighter and more elegant designs with the use of satinwood and painted decorations. (Incidentally, there is some doubt as to whether Sheraton even had a workshop or produced any of the furniture which bears his name.)

During the Regency period furniture was showing the early signs of pregnancy which were to become monstrous during Victoria's reign. Rosewood was widely used and the influence of French *Directoire* styles was felt. After Trafalgar everything became Egyptian with sphinxes' heads, claw feet and so on.

In the nineteenth century there was a heavy import tax on mahogany; which tax led to the use of wood from Honduras, both lighter and less richly coloured than the Cuban or Jamaican mahogany. Then the massive Victorian styles wallowed into fashion. There were *some* pretty Victorian chairs, balloon-backs and button-backs, but nobody would claim today that it was a golden age, at least not until the International Exhibition in London (1862) when William Morris first put his furniture on public display. He called it 'Gothic', but it wasn't like the usual 'trade' Gothic, because it was Morris's philosophy that we should clamber back into the cot of the Middle Ages and construct a Socialist Utopia in which the dignity of labour was once again respected and the craftsman could be free to develop his craft. Morris and 'The Firm' produced two classes of furniture, his 'State' furniture and his 'Cottage' style. The first attempted perfection of design, the second functionalism, a dirty word so far as most Victorians were concerned.

The Sussex Chair was typical of Morris's cottage furniture—I could have bought one for £25 at a country fair not long ago—and it was both charming and without condescension. Out of William Morris's work came the Arts and Crafts Movement of the 1880s, which re-interpreted many of the traditional English forms, notably Ernest Grimson's ladder-back chair. And hence to Art Nouveau . . .

From this brief summary (which owes a lot to Arthur Negus, a man who has the ability to make interesting things familiar and familiar things interesting), it may be seen that there were three great innovators in the history of chair manufacture, Kent, Chippendale and Morris. But there was also a continuing tradition of country craftsmen whose work, if it changed at all, changed but slowly. I am about to draw your attention to their chairs because a set of four Hepplewhites will set you back at least £250, and a set of six £500, while a single Chippendale ladder-back will cost around £75. We're in the Big Time, you see, and bargains will not be easy to find. Not that you shouldn't look, bearing in mind that the prices of chairs tend to depend on the amount of visible detail, and that age is not paramount—a good Hepplewhite is worth more than a good Chippendale, which in turn is worth more than a good Charles II chair. (If you do look, remember to check whether the seat rails have been stained or whether there is stain under the stretchers. There should be no stain. Take out any loose seats and check under the centre of the splat where the number of the chair in the set may have been carved. If this number is in Roman numerals, so far, so good. If it's in Arabic the chair is quite modern.) But bargains in country furniture may still be found.

Windsor Chairs
These attractive stick-back chairs have been made for over two hundred years and it's the old ones you should be after. They come in various designs: comb-backs, sometimes with a braced back—good news!—and saddle-seats (which all old Windsor chairs ought

Country Chair
Elm with Beech
Arms

Inlaid Bedroom
Chair

to have, especially the armchairs). Usually made of ash or elm or fruitwood, these gave place to the hoop-backs (backs and arms usually constructed of beech, which was flexible enough to make the hoops) and the wheel-backs, which have a wheel design in the central splat.

Reproduction machine-made wheel-back chairs give themselves away by the uniformity of their seats, which are scarcely shaped at all, nor do they have sufficient patina (the mysterious quality which all old furniture possesses in the same way that old men gain dignity).

Windsor chairs made out of yew with ash seats were sometimes stained a reddish-brown. These are rare and attractive, and quite valuable. Indeed all yew furniture is desirable.

Old Windsor chairs of the eighteenth century had wide seats to accommodate the voluminous clothes of the period, and their arms were cut away half-way round the seats. Eighteenth-century elm Windsor chairs will cost about £50, but the narrower nineteenth-century ones are less than half that. Sets are expensive because few have survived, and bear in mind that they still make Windsor chairs in High Wycombe.

Ladder-backs, spindle-backs, Essex chairs and Corner chairs all fetch fair prices, but Bentwood chairs (*not* invented by a Mr Bentwood—as I used rashly to claim—anyway they were all the rage in the 1870s) are still reasonably priced and attractive in their simplicity.

For £10 or less you can still get little inlaid mahogany bedroom chairs, sometimes even with turned legs; these really are bargains.

Finally, a word about *Anobium punctatum*, the furniture beetle or woodworm. He's not a mean little chap and only really likes soft woods, like politicians' heads. You will barely find him alive in old furniture; if he is, a tap on the surface of the wood with a hard object will send out little puffs of dust. Then you must steel yourself and block him in with beeswax.

When the cry of 'Worm!' goes up at an auction, as often as not it's a dealer trying to discourage competition; let your eyes be the judge, and unless the thing is riddled with worm, and unless you discover the elixir of eternal youth, it'll outlive you.

Books: *Going for a Song* by Arthur Negus and Max Robertson (BBC, 1969)
Country Furniture by Jane Toller (David and Charles, 1973)
The Windsor Chair by Ivan Sparkes (Spur Books, 1975)

China

There's a joy without canker or cark,
There's a pleasure eternally new,

'Tis to gloat on the glaze and the mark
Of china that's ancient and blue.
'Ballade of Blue China' by Andrew Lang

If in the late 1930s you had invested £18 in Royal Worcester's new Dorothy Doughty designed model of a 'Baltimore Oriole and Tulip Tree', one of her famous American bird models, you would have had cause to congratulate yourself because in 1968 such a model was sold at auction for £5,700. But if you had invested the same sum in, say, Chinese export porcelain, you would by 1968 in real money terms have shown a loss. In short, investing in china is a

Mickey Mouse
Nursery China c1930

speculative business. But if you have no intention of 'investing', you just find the prices in the shops too high, and would like to buy some pretty china for your own use or display, then, bless you, you can't go wrong. A nice old blue and white transfer pattern meat dish (Caughley, Spode, Wedgwood, Riley, Ridgeway or Rogers for choice) will cost you about £10 on my stall (and only a little more on anyone else's!) and you will have to keep and to use something old, something English, something made by craftsmen who were absolutely confident in their craft, and something which will turn a Sunday joint from a treat into a feast. (Yvonne has a theory about the popularity of blue and white china; she says that food always looks good on it because there is hardly any food which is itself blue.) Now a modern meat dish for the same price will be an infinitely less agreeable object, and that is why I insist that the old dish will be a true bargain. We have extended the principle. We eat off odd dinner plates, each one attractive in its own right, but none having cost us more than a pound or so. If we break one—and I do—there is no problem about replacement, and in brief we eat in style at a minimal cost. A bargain? I think so. Soup plates, tea-cups, saucers, plates, and coffee cups are amassed in the same way.

So you say: 'Well, that's all very well for bohemians, but we have a certain standard to keep up. If Geoffrey brings the boss home to dinner we would not want him to think we were reduced to oddments.' Very well, madam you too can benefit from this useful chapter.

The Victorians had large families, everyone knows that. Consequently they needed huge dinner services of well over a hundred pieces. Although many of these sets were later split up amongst the family, they remain large enough for families in the seventies, and can be obtained extremely cheaply by comparison with the prices of modern services in the shops. At recent auctions I have noted the following:

Dinner services
72 pieces Victorian Minton . . . £110
105 pieces of Rosenthal . . . £50 (bought by me)
44 pieces Charles Meigh . . . £100
86 pieces green and gilt pottery . . . £25
35 pieces Wedgwood Creamware . . . £75
77 pieces Coalport . . . £60
64 pieces Copeland . . . £50

Tea services
20 pieces John Roze Coalport . . . £42
25 pieces Staffordshire . . . £30

53 pieces Royal Worcester breakfast and tea service ... £28
(bought by me)
45 pieces Paragon China ... £45
30 pieces Victorian unmarked ... £9

So you say: 'Well, that's all very well, but if Geoffrey brings the boss home to dinner we don't want him to think we're Victorians. Geoffrey doesn't work in an old-fashioned firm, you know. Cringe Comptometers have a modern image, besides which our house is tremendously contemporary and always was. We have a bidet, you know, and a barbecue.' Very well, madam, only don't push me too far.

If you want to be thought to be in the swim, you can still find at reasonable prices vaguely art deco sets of china by makers like the redoubtable Susie Cooper. The late Clarice Cliff, the first exhibition of whose work has just been on view, is all the rage (especially her whimsical Bizarre range). You may still find items by her, but don't go to the shops!

'Very well, young man, but I thought this book was intended to be factual. It's all very well to speak slightingly of shops (they have to live too, you know) and boast about how clever you've been, but we don't need all that; we need *facts*.'

Well, I shan't give you many facts. The subject is far too broad to be dealt with here. But I have recommended a number of excellent specialist books on china collecting to which you can refer (see page 189). How's that, Madam? Oh, she's gone.

But one basic set of facts you do need to know. So here we go.

Pottery is the basic clay, which, when baked in the kiln, becomes **earthenware** (like flower-pots). When baked harder the clay vitrifies and becomes **stoneware**. **Porcelain** is a refined kind of stoneware, made from two kinds of felspathic rock, fused together. **Bone china**, which was evolved in Britain, notably by Josiah Spode, contains a generous admixture of bone ash and is glazed. **Stone china** is a very tough and heavy kind of stoneware and also goes under the names of ironstone, semi-china etc. For other subspecies of china (parian, bisque, slipware etc.) please consult a glossary of antiques.

Now it remains to recommend a few other areas in which bargains are to be found.

We collect little Victorian jugs, which are unpretentious and delightful. Unless you wish to buy the aristocrats (such as Worcester Chamberlain) you need never spend more than £3 for these. Doll's china is a cheap way of collecting examples of the

*Blue + White Spode Ewer
1820 – 1830*

grander styles. Copeland and Garret (late Spode) specialised in doll's china in the mid-nineteenth century. Cups and saucers with tea-pot, sugar basin and cream jug made up the set which sometimes came with a matching tray. Other doll's china (a Victorian innovation) was produced in the Ironstone, Tea Leaf and the Moss Rose patterns. And much was unmarked. Doll's china is understandably confused with travellers' samples, which were accurate models, occasionally up to half size, of real sets.

Also charming are the moralistic Victorian Staffordshire plates and mugs printed with alphabets, improving texts, wise saws and inspiring pictures, ensuring that children Knew Their Place, at mealtimes anyway. There were designs in the style of Kate Greenaway and Florence K. Upton, the Golliwog woman, and these and Beatrix Potter figures are much reproduced by contemporary potters, and make pleasant stocking-fillers.

And now for toilet sets, which originally consisted of seven pieces, but have usually been reduced to 'Js and Bs' by the time they reach the saleroom. I am amazed that there are any jugs and basins left in Britain, since close on a million have been exported.

Those that are left sell at about £12 the set, so that people can grow flowers in the jugs and drink punch out of the basins. Nice things, simple, straightforward, no better than they should be, and no worse.

So far as Staffordshire figures and 'flat-backs' are concerned, my advice is to leave them well alone. Cottages, dogs and cats, Wesleys (he visited the potteries), Princes and Princesses (vaguely modelled on Victoria and Albert), huntsmen, highlanders, frog-mugs, up they come, down goes the hammer and off they trot, and as many of them are modern as are old, and I should never feel confident, if I paid over the odds for one, that I hadn't made a fool of myself. But I must emphasize, yet again, that if you like them and they seem reasonably priced to you, buy them, why not, and what's it matter, if they give pleasure to you, what snotty-nosed experts think or say?

Other attractive items at modest prices which I have found especially popular on my stall are:

Souvenir China. 'Presents from' cups and saucers and mugs with the name of the resort in gilt gothic lettering sell for about £1·50. Coronation and Jubilee mugs are pricier, especially if they come from the Doulton factory, so that a Doulton Victoria Jubilee mug will sell for about £6, but a George VI Coronation mug, unmarked, should be a mere £2·50 or so.

Ribbon Plates. Plates with pierced edges and frequently a central floral design are snapped up at £5. If you happen upon an early Leeds creamware ribbon plate, you have found yourself a treasure. They are delightful but expensive.

Quimper. My friend Gill Levy snaps up all the Quimper pieces I get for *her* friend, so I have been on the look-out for them, and very pretty they are too with their bright colours and whimsical shapes and designs. Expect to pay on average £3 per item.

Footwarmers. These came after warming pans but before the rubbery things which leak. Being stoneware they are extremely heavy and tend to have patent numbers and maker's names scrawled all over them. Sullen things, but they do retain the heat, and cost about £2·50.

Cow-creamers. I have never felt the same about cow-creamers since I read *The Code of the Woosters*: 'When I say cow don't go running away with the idea of some decent, self-respecting cudster such as you may observe loading grass into itself in the nearest meadow. This was a sinister, leering, Underworld sort of animal, the kind that would spit out of the side of its mouth for twopence.' Of course, what Aunt Dahlia was after was a silver cow-creamer, but little china cow-creamers are much nastier and much more readily

18th Century Blue + White Cow Creamer

available. They are not all nasty, the blue and white ones with windmills all over them are quite sweet, though not very bovine, and in any case people always want to buy them at £5 or £10.

There are many other bits and pieces which I have no space to detail here, nor need I, since you will discover them for yourself and half the pleasure will be in the discovery, but I should say a word about the better stuff.

You may find by accident or by design that you are the owner of a fine old piece of china, whose quality is self-evident. Check the mark in a book like Chaffers' classic *Collector's Handbook of*

Marks on Pottery and Porcelain and, if you can identify it, that will give you some idea as to its value. If it's old and from one of the famous firms, then it's sure to be worth a bit. And even if it doesn't carry a mark of any kind that need not distress you. Not all potters marked all their wares. And if you need to know more about your prize, take it to the curator of your local museum or to the biggest dealer in your neighbourhood, or to the Victoria and Albert on a Tuesday or Thursday afternoon. Everyone likes to be asked for his or her professional opinion, so don't be shy. And unless you need to sell—having established that it *is* Chelsea or Derby or Bow or whatever—don't. It's sure to prove a sound investment.

If the subject of china intrigues and attracts you (as it does me) never miss an opportunity to go round a museum where there is a display or, if you find yourself in Worcester, visit the Royal Worcester factory (a guided tour is only 40p and the museum is enchanting); familiarise yourself whenever possible with the look and the feel of old porcelain. Then specialise in that which appeals most energetically to you. Good luck.

Books: *English Pottery and Porcelain* by W. B. Honey (Black, 1969)
Price Guide to 18th Century English Porcelain by Simon Spero (Antique Collectors Club, 1976)
Price Guide to 19th and 20th Century British Porcelain by David Battie and Michael Turner (Antique Collectors Club, 1975)
Porcelain by John Cushion (Orbis Publications, 1973)
Pocket Book of English Ceramic Marks by J. P. Cushion (Faber, 1965)
Illustrated Guide to British Pottery and Porcelain by Geoffrey A. Godden (Barrie & Jenkins, 1970).

(These are on the general subject of china. For a detailed bibliography see page 189.)

Cigarette Cards (Cartophily)

A cigarette is the perfect type of a perfect pleasure. It is exquisite, and it leaves one unsatisfied. What more can one want?
     The Picture of Dorian Gray by Oscar Wilde

Cigarette cards developed one hundred years ago from trade-cards. The best examples are pre-1902, when the large tobacco combines came into being, but the craze was at its height between 1920 and 1940, when some three hundred million were printed annually. Gold Flake and Black Cat and Cadbury's were very prolific, but the smaller company's cards of the pre-1920s, such as John Sinclair of Newcastle and Taddy of London, are better investments; indeed their prices have bounded ahead during the last few years. Since the last war an agreement by the manufacturers not to continue with the cards was broken by Players with their recent series in Donicella Cigars. And since the 1950s Brooke Bond has included cards in their tea-packets.

Gallahers 1936

His late Majesty King Edward VII

Players 1911

As with postage stamps good condition is essential. Amongst the early cards the royals and the military are particularly popular; amongst the later cards transport, national flags and uniforms should be tracked down. But really the fanaticism is such that anything will be wanted by somebody. One wonders whether Green Shield stamps will ever be collected with such fervour (but of course they already are!).

At auction recently a single card dated 1898 (A Jones' 'Portrait of Victoria') fetched £18, a set of 50 silhouettes of warships, dated 1915, went for £26, and a set of 25 cinema stars from the '30s went for £9. If this seems steep then you ought to know that the record is some £2,000 for the series 'Clowns and Various Artists'.

But why go on? Far better subscribe to *Cigarette Card News* or invest in one or more of the catalogues produced by the amazing London Cigarette Card Company. This organization has a stock of 200 million cards, and catalogued lists of just about every card ever issued, both singly and in sets. They have also published a useful booklet, *Collecting Cigarette Cards* by Dorothy Bagnall (1973).

Clocks

Then came, at a predetermined moment, a moment in time and of time,
A moment not out of time, but in time, in what we call history:
transecting, bisecting the world of time, a moment in time but not like a moment of time,
A moment in time but time was made through that moment: for without the meaning there is no time, and that moment of time gave the meaning.

'The Rock' by T. S. Eliot

You won't be able to buy a grandfather clock in working order for less than £150, and there's a simple reason for this. You can spot them a mile off. That's their charm of course, but you're not likely to find one hidden under a pile of junk, nor in a job lot, nor in a junky antique shop. Everyone knows that long-case clocks (that's what you must call them now, just as you must talk about a 'projection' when you mean a guess and a 'scenario' when you mean a plan) are worth money, so sadly, I must exclude them from this bargain-obsessed book. On the other hand if you chance to find one with the names of Tompion or Quare or East or Graham or Knibb on it, well you might safely bid a few hundred. And on the *other* hand, there is a man turning out reproduction clocks for round about £100, but you wouldn't want one of those, surely, would you, seeing that you're people of taste and discernment!

Let us instead consider some of the clocks that others less discerning and tasteful than yourselves may have passed over.

Carriage Clocks
These are usually cased in brass, and often have an additional leather case into which they slide cosily. They have a small handle

on the top and few of them have ever seen the inside of a carriage. Fact is, they were travelling clocks, designed to travel both from place to place and from room to room. The real carriage and sedan-chair clocks were like large watches, framed and ringed.

Perhaps I shouldn't be wasting your time with all this chat about carriage clocks, since these, like grandfather clocks, tend not to get overlooked. Forty pounds is the least I've seen one sell for, a charming French one it was too, in a rosewood and floral marquetry inlaid case. Of course the 'carriage clock' you can purchase with your Green Shield stamps sells for less, but the less said about them the better!

Where you may find a real bargain (a sound attractive clock at a price hugely lower than that of a modern equivalent) is in the area of American clocks, Postman's clocks and Mantel clocks.

American Clocks

The typical American clock, which was cheap enough to be imported into this country some 150 years ago at a price which struck terror into the escapement of every British clock-maker and made his dial turn pale, came in a hanging case about a foot and a half high, glass-fronted and with a coloured print below the clock-face. They were not of high quality, with working parts as often as not made of wood, but they had charm and have even down the years acquired a little distinction; and what's more to the point, they can still be picked up for £15–£20, sometimes less.

Postman's Clocks

If you are not keen on things American, then you could consider what I call Postman's Clocks. By this I mean those attractive circular or octagonal wall clocks with handsome mahogany frames and nice clear black numbers. These currently fetch from £40 and look just right in a country kitchen. A lot of them started their working lives in kitchens, I fancy, there not being enough postmen to go round. Large postmen's clocks about two foot in diameter were probably hung as advertisements by coaching inns when the clock tax of 1797 made clocks and watches too expensive for ordinary folk.

Mantel Clocks

Mantel clocks may be bought even more cheaply. A Victorian or Edwardian balloon clock in inlaid mahogany, an artefact elegant

American Clock
1800 - 1830

Inlaid Mantel
Clock

enough to grace any mantelpiece in the land, may be had for the cost of a return rail ticket to Birmingham.

Then there are the heavy slate German mantel clocks and the French ones with gilded metal and Sèvres porcelain panels (which you'll not find so easy to acquire) and the art deco ones which told the time *so* slowly between the air raid warning and the all clear, and a thousand other sorts, all for far less than you would pay for a piece of modern tat. You'll not know till you get them home whether or not they work (they usually do if they come from an 'effects' auction, don't if they come from 'trade'). But, even if they don't, they are precisely right twice in every twenty-four hours which is *something* to be proud of.

Books: *Craft of the Clockmaker* by E. J. Tyler (Ward Lock, 1973)
Repairing Antique Clocks, a guide for amateurs by Eric P. Smith (David & Charles, 1973)
Country Clocks and Their London Origins by Brian Loomes (David & Charles, 1976)

Britten's Old Clocks and Watches and Their Makers, 8th edition revised and enlarged by Cecil Clutton (Eyre Methuen, 1973)

Coins

Whoso has sixpence is sovereign (to the length of sixpence) over all men; commands cooks to feed him, philosophers to teach him, kings to mount guard over him—to the length of sixpence.

Past and Present by Thomas Carlyle

There are over one hundred clubs and societies for people who collect coins in the United Kingdom alone (and I mean collect coins for the things themselves and not for exchange). There are twice that number of full-time dealers. There are magazines such as *Coins and Medals, Coin Monthly* and *Coins, Medals and Currency*. Yet, despite the vast amount of specialisation—and if you feel numismatical and take up numismatics, you really ought to specialise, otherwise you will drown in a tidal wave of dates and currencies and metals—it is still possible to make a killing. Mr Horace Burrows of Chelmsford did. He checked his change and discovered a 1952 halfcrown, hitherto and since unrecorded. It was sold for £2,000 to America. Since decimalisation you are no longer likely to find a halfcrown in your change—indeed since inflation went mad you are unlikely to have any change—but in other ways decimalisation has given British coin collecting a boost. When in 1967 it was announced that no more halfpennies were to be minted, competition for £5 bags of newly-minted halfpennies became so savage that they were being offered at £11. The bubble burst when the Mint announced that they were to resume minting the halfpenny, so that now the 1967 coin is quite commonplace. But brass threepenny pieces of 1946 and 1949 are worth at least £15 and £30 respectively in 'uncirculated' condition, while uncirculated sixpences of 1942, '46, '52, '54, and '55 are all worth having. The years for pennies are 1895 (old heads as opposed to bun pennies), 1912, '22, '32, '33, '34, '51 and—not that you'll find one—1954. You see, the whole mystique of coin collecting is that value is in proportion to rarity and mintage, with aesthetics trailing in a long way last. There is not even a very great element of risk because silver coins have a scrap value based on the current price of silver; coins minted before 1947 contain half silver, and those minted before 1920 contain $92\frac{1}{2}\%$ of silver. And gold sovereigns, worth about £45 as I write, half-sovereign, about £33, and crowns, about £10, obviously depend upon the spot rate of gold.

There are more romantic areas to explore, and, were I a numismatist, I should pay a call on W. H. Lane and Sons of Penzance who specialise in auctioning what is salvaged from shipwrecks. On 26 September 1975 they auctioned the salvage from no fewer than nine shipwrecks, pieces of eight predominating. (Without sal-

Threepence

Sovereign 1901–1910

Half Sovereign 1834

vage and treasure trove, the laws appertaining to which are extremely confusing and should be carefully noted, the coin-collecting industry would rapidly disappear.)

Should you chance upon a Victorian gold £5 piece amongst your shopping, consider yourself lucky. I need do no more than quote from the priced catalogue of a Hove auctioneer:

'Victoria Gold Five Pounds 1887 variety without initials on reverse (extremely rare virtually FDC)—£1850.
Victoria Gold Five Pounds 1839, Una and the Lion type with two decorated fillets, one with six scrolls, the other eleven leaves, the edge inscribed between wine edge raised rims (very rare, a few slight scratches, otherwise FDC)—£4,500.'

I suppose there is a kind of poetry to be found there.

Book: *Collecting Coins* by P. Frank Purvey (Gifford, 1971)

100

Copper and Brass

> *Some minds improve by travel; others rather*
> *Resemble copper wire, or brass,*
> *Which get the narrower by going farther.*
> Thomas Hood

From my carrel (the word is derived from its meaning of a monastic cell) in Sutton Library I have a charming view of the local church. I stare out of the window at the church steeple, atop of which perches ... a copper cock. (Some say the reason cocks were put on church steeples was in awful memory of St Peter; others simply that the wind catches the tail feathers, and that it acts more effectively as a weather-vane than other designs.)

Copper kettle 1820

Copper was a most useful ancient metal. It was mixed with tin to form bronze, and with zinc to form brass, although a few hundred years ago 'brass' and 'bronze' were used vaguely for any kind of copper alloy.

The most attractive copper items to collect are kitchen utensils, pots and pans, kettles, fire-irons and so forth. An antique copper preserving pan will set you back about £25 (the same thing in brass will be just half that). Then there are candlesticks (an average of about £20 a pair for brass ones), door knockers and hand warmers.

Warming pans are quite interesting and frequently appear on the market. Early ones had long steel handles and brass faces with a lid which much overhung the base (and hence the erroneous story of James II's heir being smuggled into the Palace in a warming pan, whereas you and I know that he was found under a gooseberry bush like the rest of us).

In the eighteenth and early nineteenth centuries copper was the most popular metal for warming pans, and by now the lid fitted snugly. Later on, in the nineteenth century, the lid was joined to the pan, and it became the practice to fill it with water in place of embers—since kitchens now had ranges this was obviously convenient. At the end of the last century the warming pan yielded to the foot-warmer, which in time made way for rubber hot-water bottles and electric blankets. I've tried them all and, believe me, dogs are best.

If you want to buy a warming pan, it's advisable to study the handle with particular care. It should be well-turned and tight-fitting—fruitwood probably. Look carefully at the copper pan too; the engraving should not be too bright and unworn. There are many reproductions on the market. Average prices for genuine ones are £30 for brass and £45 for copper.

What else in brass and copper could you collect? Almost anything. Chestnut roasters (about £10) are agreeable both for decoration and for nuts; door-knockers, though much reproduced, are not without glamour. Copper coal helmets and brass log baskets, brass fenders (£20) and pestles and mortars (£15), antique door-stops, water jugs, tobacco tampers, trivets, scales and weights, old instruments . . . it's a long list.

Horse brasses are fun. They have talismanic properties, like the spike on the head of the charger and the ceremonial plumes. They are at their most desirable when still attached to the leathers, and obviously old ones are weightier and more sharply cut than effete modern tat. European brasses display fertility symbols (wheatsheaf, sun and moon) but British brasses are more varied and ornamental.

Or you could collect shell-cases or beer-mullers or oil lamps or toasting forks (the extendable ones are preferable) or plaques or . . .

Brass warming pans

Book: *Collecting Copper and Brass* by Geoffrey Wills (Mayflower, 1970)

Dolls

> *Because the priest must have like every dog his day*
> *Or keep us all awake with baying at the moon,*
> *We and our dolls being but the world were best away.*
> W. B. Yeats

Having toys or dolls on my stall is a heart-breaking business. If you set your prices in accordance with what you think your goods are worth you may interest the dealers, but you'll frighten off the children. If you set your prices in accordance with what the children can afford, they'll be happy, but you'll be bankrupt. I try to solve the problem by having two sets of prices, one for dealers and one for children (similarly with toy soldiers). But I sometimes find that the children are acting as runners for the dealers!

My salvation is that the early dolls were never intended as play-things. They were ornamental nonsenses. Very early dolls were the pedlar dolls, made out of wood or wax and known as slit-heads. I apologize for the phrase, but sadly doll-people use no chivalry in referring to the objects of their affection, and a 'slit-head' was a doll whose hair was inserted into her scalp through slits. (The opposite of a slit-head is a squash-head, which is a doll whose head and hair have been moulded together.) Slit-heads tend to suffer premature cracking, which makes them appear as though they have a chronic skin condition. Consequently prices for these dolls are not particularly high. The pedlar doll is of moderate interest, but its value increases with the variety and quality of goods offered in its little tray (see page 174).

When children were permitted to play with dolls, they were usually given a wood or rag doll for weekdays and a porcelain-headed doll for Sunday use. In the 1820s the wax doll was introduced as a compromise, and became instantly successful. But it wasn't until the 1850s that Augusta Montanari and her son Richard Napoleon showed what could be done with dolls and, applying the callous brutality that great artists need to survive in a Philistine world, inserted the doll's hairs, one at a time, into its head with the aid of hot needles. Augusta walked off with all the prizes at the Great Exhibition, but she asked 5 guineas for her undressed dolls, and at that price there were not too many takers. The Montanari doll is notable for its realistic flesh colours, its short neck and its stuffed linen body to which chubby limbs are sewn. But the Pierotti dolls, manufactured for a hundred and fifty years from 1780, are puce-tinted and blue-eyed. The only British doll-maker in the reckoning is Charles Marsh, whose late nineteenth-century Nordic dolls were gloriously crowned with mohair or human hair.

But none of these dolls is half as common as the eighteenth- and nineteenth-century German dolls with bisque heads attached to bodies of composition and wood.

The Germans had a monopoly of porcelain doll's heads in the mid-nineteenth century. So attractive and so cheap were they that the French factories were reduced to buying German heads and attaching them to French bodies. The faces of the German dolls were full of character, and quite accomplished. They whistled, or they ogled, or they had eyes which closed automatically by counter-weights, or they were black. The Simon and Halbig dolls, which

Bisque Doll c1910

Pegwood Doll
Late 19th Century

carry an S & H mark after 1875, were multi-racial, wore national costumes, sometimes boasted pierced ears and primitive voice-boxes.

The French responded to the German challenge with double-faced dolls, talking dolls, sucking dolls, walking dolls, dolls with teeth, and even dolls which appeared to breathe. The most cele-brated French doll is the Jumeau doll, and the most sought after Jumeau doll is one with a long face and a closed mouth. But there is a nasty habit amongst people who should know better of calling all sorts of dolls 'Jumeaus', whether there is evidence for doing so or not. In fact to the initiated the Bru doll is the more remarkable.

Dave, who collects dolls and knows about such things, is some-what cynical about marks and makes and dates. He says that his fancy is for ugly dolls and dolls with plenty of personality—and certainly many of the early slit-heads look as though they could eat the pretty Victorian dolls for breakfast and spit out the eye-balls. If I were a doll-man, I should incline more, I think, to old golliwogs, whose vogue began when Florence Upton's book *The Adventures of Two Dutch Dolls and a Golliwog* was published, and to old teddies. Teddies can take it. They are the world's punch-bags. With dolls, children have to take care, and consequently grow up full of a repressed desire to break open the china heads of their prettier friends. But those who have had teddies are relaxed and sunny and dress casually, and (except for Sir John Betjeman) don't get on much in the world but *don't care*.

Prices of dolls vary enormously. You can still buy a Victorian china doll for £30, although anything with an identifiable mark will cost considerably more.

The South East is thick with Doll and Toy Museums (Pollock's, Syon Park, Penshurst Park, etc.) and the Doll Club of Great Britain may be contacted at Grove House, Iffley Turn, Oxford.

But a word of warning. Don't try to restore or repair your dolls yourself, unless you are quite confident that you know what you are doing. And *never* use Araldite to stick wigs or limbs back on. And don't assume that a doll's hospital will necessarily do what's best for your doll. The safest thing to do is to ask a reputable doll-dealer (there's one in Camden Passage) for advice.

Books: *Collector's Encyclopaedia of Dolls* by Dorothy S. Coleman (Hale, 1970)
       Dolls by Antonia Fraser (Octopus Books, 1973)

Fakes

> *O hateful error, melancholy's child!*
> *Why dost thou show, to the apt thoughts of men,*
> *The things that are not?*
>   *Julius Caesar* by William Shakespeare

Hugo Russell & Co. has a large and well-lit warehouse just around the corner from the Transport Caff and the cheap tyre place on the road between Richmond and East Sheen. It's supposed to be for the trade only, but if you ring the bell, they may let you have a look round. 'We are manufacturers and wholesalers to the trade only of Antiques . . .', and that includes over fifty lines, from Toby jugs to horse brasses, from maps to coal helmets, from warming pans to pewter and model boats. I was very impressed with the ship's decanters from £2·50 each.

'They fetch a lot at auctions,' I said to Richard, the big, hearty guide.

'Certainly do, chief. The record so far is £128, and what particularly pleased me was that it was two dealers bidding against each other!'

But it is an alarming and salutary experience to see and touch and smell so many items which are not antiques but ought to be.

Here we enter a world of semantics, because while a forgery is a work of art made for fraudulent purposes, a fake (originally thieves' slang) is a genuine work altered in some way to give it greater desirability. And many of Hugo Russell's pieces come into a third category, called reproductions.

And now we enter a world of metaphysics. Does it matter whether the warming pan is old? Surely if you think it is, that's just as good. Maybe if you think hard enough it will become old. And in the meantime you can buy it quite cheaply.

But if you are worried about the genuineness of some 'antique', what can you do about it? Well you can always demand your money back, since antique dealers are subject to the Trades Description Act, just as any other retailers are. But it will strengthen your hand enormously if you obtain from the vendor a written description of the piece, so that, if it is shown to be erroneous, you have the law on your side. (In my experience all you usually need do is ask for your money back and you'll get it.) But it does help to avoid any embarrassment if you know in advance the sort of goods which are currently being reproduced, forged and faked. At once you discover that many things must be genuine simply because it would cost a lot more to make copies. Here we have stumbled upon a great truth; no one is going to bother to forge something of little intrinsic value, and no one is going to be able profitably to forge something of enormous manufactured complexity.

However, since the price of antiques has increased so rapidly in the past few years, it has now become worthwhile faking things in the modest price range of, say, £10–£50, and indeed this is where most of the action is. The police are not going to worry too much about a set of horse brasses, so that distribution will be no problem: nothing easier with all these antiques fairs about.

Here is a short list of a few of the things which are least frequently what they seem: cased glass (coloured overlay with cutaway designs) comes from the Chinese People's Republic; pistols and long guns, especially those with percussion actions, are coming on to the market from North Africa: wholesale they're some £8 each, but in the saleroom at least £30; pewter, which is reputably advertised as having 'genuine William and Mary touch-marks', is very vulnerable: remember that though touch-marks may legally be punched, revenue marks on measures may *not* be; Dutch Delft and Maiolica are manufactured in Holland, while Staffordshire figures and animals are still made by the same processes and sometimes in the same potteries as their aged predecessors—does this make them fakes?; 'Rockingham' pastille burners, sheep, etc. are imported very cheaply from Spain, while Lustreware (especially the copper-coloured items) and Toby jugs and frog-mugs are hardly ever as old as they profess to be. Beware too of Mary Gregory glass, Fabergé eggs, potlids, oil lamps, ship's trunks, doorstops and coal helmets.

Indeed it is a jungle, and the only precautions you can take are to familiarise yourself with what the real article looks like. Haunt the Wallace Collection. Browse at the Victoria & Albert Museum. Try and handle things as much as possible. *Never* buy when you feel suspicious and try to avoid the most frequently faked items. You are less likely to find non-genuine pieces in an auction of effects than in an auction of trade goods or bankrupt stock. Buy only—and this is the golden rule—what you really like and what can't cheaply be copied.

And if, like the rest of us, you do make a fool of yourself, console yourself with this thought: We are all reproductions.

Books: *How to Detect Fake Antiques* by John Fitzmaurice Mills
(Arlington Books, 1972)
Fakes by O. Kurz (Dover, 1968)

Fans

For you muddled with books and pictures, an' china an' etchin's an' fans,
And your rooms at college was beastly—more like a whore's than a man's.

'The Mary Gloster' by Rudyard Kipling

I don't like having fans on my stall. Children can't resist fans, and I can resist children. Children who will play with my fans and pop their bubblegum at the same time are easy to resist. Fans are not

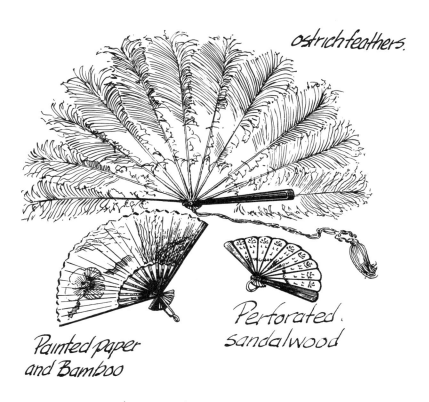

ostrich feathers.

*Painted paper
and Bamboo*

*Perforated
sandalwood*

French Lace Fan 1860-70

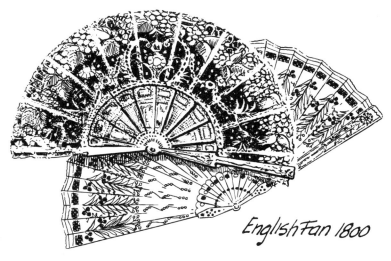

English Fan 1800

robust. I consequently price mine low (about £1 a throw) and hope that they'll survive.

Fans were popular in the East thousands of years ago, but it wasn't till the late sixteenth century that the Portuguese traders brought fans to Europe. The early European ones were Chinese in style, ornately carved and with scenes painted across the leaves of chicken-skin parchment. Brisés were fans with stick-leaves painted or incised or threaded with ribbons.

But it was the Victorians who made fans fun. The Regency silks gave way to lace (Honiton and Brussels for white lace, Chantilly for black). Sticks and mounts were of mother-of-pearl, ivory or tortoise-shell. You could have monograms or jewels or matching parasols. You would certainly have a satin-lined box, tooled in gold or silver. You could even have for ballroom use a fan with a spy-hole in the guard to help you decide in plenty of time whether you wished to remain a wallflower.

In 1876 there was a fan exhibition in South Kensington (where else?). Rex Whistler went and decided that fans made suitable wall-decorations. After which you could hardly move for the things. Huge ostrich-feather fans, pretty tambour fans which opened when you pulled a cord in the handle, black mourning fans inlaid with mother-of-pearl.

But then towards the end of the century the fans lost their flamboyance and became decadent. They had designs on them mass-produced from printing-plates. They were used to advertise trades people and manufacturers. Queen Victoria was not amused.

For a Victorian lace fan expect to pay upwards of £6, and for an ostrich-feather one a little more. For Regency fans, £50 would be a fair average price, but that's getting out of our class, and the kids would surely choose *that* one to wipe their sticky fingers on.

Book: *Collector's History of Fans* by Nancy Armstrong (Studio Vista, 1974)

Furniture

A man should keep his little brain attic stocked with all the furniture that he is likely to use, and the rest he can put away in the lumber-room of his library, where he can get it if he wants it.
        The Five Orange Pips by Sir Arthur Conan Doyle

I mean, the question is, have you good taste? And if you have, you'll know what *quality* is all about without my explaining it to you. And, if you have not (and it's one of those things which your best friends won't tell you) you're not going magically to acquire it on the strength of a thousand words from my canary-yellow Bic ballpoint pen.

Shaw reviled good taste as lack of originality, and one can see his point. After all, the good taste of a middle-class late Victorian family, to whom good taste was paramount, is today considered to be the essence of vulgarity, but in the matter of buying bargains in old furniture you may not live long enough to see your 'originality' officially approved, nor your 'good taste' go out of fashion. And bargains are there to be bought.

And the next question is, will a little knowledge help you to recognise these bargains? In Ernle Bradford's book *Antique Furniture* he warns us always to bear in mind that a little learning is a dangerous thing, but coincidentally Plantagenet Somerset Fry in *his* book *Antique Furniture* argues: 'While it takes years to become an expert in any one field, I am inclined to think that a little learn-

Oak Farmhouse Refectory Table

Georgian Mahogany Drop Leaf Table

ing in the antique field is not so dangerous a thing as it may be elsewhere.'

Bradford or Fry? I incline to Fry. After all, if a very clever craftsman sets out to deceive you, you will be, I will be, deceived—but we can't be *very* deceived if we don't pay *very* much. And modern furniture has become so expensive that even doctored antiques are worth buying.

Take tables. You can buy a nice little eighteenth-century elm table for £40—about the same as you might expect to pay for a Victorian walnut table, or a set of six Victorian kitchen chairs (though I have dealt with chairs in greater detail elsewhere). Wardrobes, even pleasantly proportioned, bow-fronted ones with claw feet and mother-of-pearl on their handles can be purchased for under £50, and little open bookcases with inlay decoration can be found at less than £20.

Footstools, which came into popular prominence with the Victorian fashion for stately pregnancies, are readily available decorated with beadwork or needlework. Many of these are beautifully elegant (particularly the Regency pieces which are not so easy to come by) and ideal for children to sit on while watching television. The narrow fender-stools, four foot long and traditionally decorated with lilies, are the next most useful article of furniture after the bed.

There's scarcely anything which cannot be found at an auction; music cabinets, standard lamps, *torchères* or plant stands, cake stands (ideal for displaying trinkets), linen presses, bureaux (which *are* pricey, I'm afraid), settees, chaises longues and even three-piece suites. If you are lucky enough to live in a castle, or anywhere with echoing spaces to fill, you will be particularly favoured because it is the huge items which nobody wants, vast old chests and armchairs and hall-stands and mirrors. But large oak pieces, and especially antique oak—are energetically hunted down by continental dealers who can never get enough of this particular wood. South Coast and East Anglian auctioneers pander to this all-consuming passion; if you want oak, go West or North, young man!

One can learn a certain amount from books, but a visit to a good furniture museum is worth a hundred chapters. In London the Victoria and Albert (of course) and the Geffrye Museum are recommended (the Wallace Collection is strong in French pieces), and in Birmingham Aston Hall and in Leeds Temple Newsam House should be patronised.

Turn of the century Bookcase

You may find signs of woodworm in your furniture, but, although some regard these tiny holes with the same sort of horror they would only otherwise display at syphilitic symptoms in their grandparents, there is really no need. In spring or early summer when the beetles breed, you may find these tell-tale puffs of powdered wood (particularly in walnut and other soft woods and in glued plywood which you should banish from any home with old furniture in it). Then you must protect your eyes and attack with an aerosol spray. Fill the holes with plastic wood—or sawdust and paste which you can stain with pigment until it matches the wood to be treated—clean the surface, and wax-polish it with one of the polishes which contains anti-woodworm ingredients.

If the article is of no great value and is in poor condition, you may apply a commercial paint stripper (taking care to protect your hands and eyes—indeed this is a job best done in the garden) with cottonwool or a brush. After allowing time for the stripper to act, white spirit should be applied to remove all traces of stripper, varnish, polish, paint, and finger-ends. (To be on the safe side I suggest you sign on for a course in furniture restoration at your adult education college!)

And finally remember the damaging effect of central heating on valuable old furniture. A hydrometer to record the humidity in the room and a humidifier to stabilise it would prove wise investments.

Books: *Country Furniture* by Jane Toller (David & Charles, 1973)

Antique Furniture by Ernle Bradford (Teach Yourself Books, 1970)

Antique Furniture by Plantagenet Somerset Fry (Hamlyn Paperbacks, 1972)

Going For a Song by Arthur Negus and Max Robertson (BBC Publications, 1969)

Antique Furniture for the Smaller Home by Peter Philip (Arco, 1962)

Beginner's Guide to Collecting Antique Furniture by Patrick MacNaughton (Pelham, 1973)

Glass

And nothing to say and the glasses are raised, we are happy
Drinking through time, and a world that is gentle and helpless
Survives in the pub and goes up in the smoke of our breath,
The regulars doze in the corner, the talkers are fluent;
Look now in the faces of those you love and remember
That you are not thinking of death.

'Pub' by Julian Symons

Glass is to china as Bach is to Beethoven, and the collector of drinking glasses is a Preludes and Fugues man. There are numerous parallels. Bach's *Klavier* was well-tempered, so is old glass. The changes which Bach rings (glass rings too!) on just a few variables, rhythms and harmonies and chord sequences, are as elaborate and inventive as the changes which the glassmakers rang on bowls and stems and feet. There are even talented musicians today making music on glass tubes, and very haunting and ethereal it is too.

George Ravenscroft (1618–1681) was the J. S. Bach of glass. He it was who took glass-making away from the Venetians. He obtained the requisite silica from English flints and added as his secret ingredient an oxide of lead, called litharge. The results were superb. His glass was heavy and brilliant and light was refracted from it as if from the haloes of a throng of saints. Ravenscroft and his successors produced the finest glass ever made in this country—a golden age, but a brief one.

The eighteenth century produced the Jacobite glasses in which were commemorated and from which was drunk the health of the Young Pretender. The symbols are all there, a rose with one or two buds, an oak leaf and a thistle, a portrait of one of the two Pretenders, verses from Jacobite ballads, royal crowns, stars, the cipher I.R. (for James Rex) incorporating the number 8, the messages 'Fiat', 'Redeat', 'Health to all our fast friends', or the less stirring 'Amen'.

Amen glasses are the most desired of all Jacobite glasses, but have been extensively (and often successfully) forged. They were made from 1747 for a small group of Jacobite V.I.P.s and contain engraved upon them verses of Jacobite hymns ending with the word 'Amen'.

Contemporary with these are the Williamite glasses probably made for the fiftieth anniversary of the Battle of the Boyne. On these you may find an Irish harp, an Orange Order toast, a reference to the Boyne, and possibly William on horseback.

In 1745 an excise duty was imposed on glass and, since the fine related to the weight of the glass, the lead content was thereafter reduced so that facet-cutting of the new thin glass was only possible on the stems. (In Ireland there was no such duty until 1825, and in consequence the Waterford factories benefited from an influx of English talent.) So cutting was out and engraving was in, and at the end of the century the celebrated Sunderland glasses (originally representing the opening of the bridge across the Tyne in 1796, but later commemorating naval victories as well) made their appearance. These now fetch about £40 each, although not all of them are as old as their owners might claim.

How do you recognise old glass? You can examine the colour. The higher the lead content the darker the glass, and Waterford glass is very greyish. You must expect to find a large and roughened punty or pontil mark on the base of the glass. You should look for the multiple scratches which will indicate that the glass has been lowered on to a table many millions of times. On a genuinely old glass these scratches, examined under a lens, will appear to run higgledy-piggledy in all directions; on a forged glass the scratches will have some sort of artificial pattern. On old engraved glasses

18th Century
Baluster Stem
Wine Glass

Large Engraved
Wine Glass

expect to find some evidence of wear on the engraved designs. Now where was I?

In 1845 the tax on glass was finally removed and the manufacturers, who had become quite expert—if somewhat pedestrian—in engraving, faced a new threat in coloured glass from Bohemia. Well, we had our own Bristol glass of a rich, deep blue and the whimsicalities of the Nailsea designs—walking sticks and bells and rolling pins with whorls and swirls of colour.

Then the Victorians demanded sumptuous and sparkling glass, so 'rock crystal', which permitted a high polish and deep engraving, was developed. As in the other arts William Morris, influenced by Ruskin's *Stones of Venice* determined to return to the traditional English forms and Philip Webb was commissioned to design some elegant wine glasses and tumblers. These were the precursors of our familiar modern styles.

Now you'll want to know about dates and things, and it is quite possible to date your glasses by the shape of the stem, the bowl and the feet. But I'm not going to do it, not here, for it's extremely complicated. The stems are classified by names such as Balustroid and Silesian, so are the knops on the stems (Annulated, Cushion, etc.), so are the bowls (Ogee, Trumpet, Bell, etc.) and the feet (Beehive, Domed, Stepped, etc.). Correlating all these variables,

Bristol Blue
Pint Decanter
c/790

Early Victorian Heavy
Glass Decanter

your glass expert will tell you that he can't *precisely* date your glass, though near as dammit; if you don't have a tame expert, most books on glass (see below) will include a dating chart. You will find explained in them such terms as Ratafias and Rummers and Cordials. A simple test of the quality of a glass is to flick the rim with your finger-nail (*gently*) and listen to it sing; the purer the song (this is not so with opera singers, but that's another story), the purer the singer. But as with so many things the only way to learn about glass is to be near it, handle it, have it.

You are likely to come across many decanters in your bargain-hunting, and must learn to distinguish between the different periods (an excellent survey is contained in *English Antiques*, compiled and edited by G. E. Speck and Euan Sutherland). Prices vary tremendously, from about £2 for a nasty moulded modern one to about £30 for a heavily cut, spherical, long-necked Victorian one, and upwards for earlier decanters. However, it is vitally important that you check for damage before buying: it's not always easy to spot amongst the ins and outs of an elaborate example. And very probably you will find that the stopper is not the original matching stopper you thought it was, but a ground-down stopper which is of a similar pattern or a near miss. This need not worry you so much, and I always keep a wide selection of stoppers on my stall (50p to £2·25) for those in need of fitting.

Heavy cut-glass ashtrays, which were used to put under the legs of pianos to protect the carpet, are also easy to sell at £1–£2, as are vinaigrettes and silver-ended scent bottles (£9) and inkwells.

Somewhat grander and more expensive (£180 for a cameo vase, £380 for a perfume burner) are objects made of Gallé glass. But if you have the cash, it's an impeccable investment.

Emile Gallé (1846–1904) lived at Meisenthal, where his father made china, glass and furniture. He made his reputation at the

Gallé Glass Bowl.
1899

Tiffany Vase

various Paris expositions with his reinterpretation of the art forms of medieval Europe and Japan. His knowledge of horticulture was also turned to good advantage. He frequently produced (like the Jacobites) glasses upon which he engraved lines of poetry—these he called his 'verreries parlantes'. The best of his work was produced in the 1880s, and after 1889, when he started signing his pieces, his invention faltered. Nonetheless since the last war he has been increasingly and often indiscriminately in vogue.

Réné Lalique's elegant smokey glass, large plates, bowls and vases with naked nymphs and waving reeds and things, is also much collected, and there are plenty of minor pieces around at endurable prices to reward the collector. Lalique's car mascots particularly seen suddenly to have become irresistible.

Louis Comfort Tiffany was a contemporary of Gallé, and very much his trans-Atlantic equivalent, since he too revolutionised glass design. Tiffany characteristics are peacock feathers, leaves and Japanese style patterns frequently in his own patented (1880) iridescent glass. He is in the mainstream of Art Nouveau. Like Gallé he continued to produce in his declining years, and had many imitators, notably J. Lötz Witwe of Klostermühle.

You'll be lucky to find any genuine Tiffany piece for less than £200, and his lamps fetch £4,000 and over. Agreeably decorative Tiffany-style lamps at a hundredth of that price are available at Christopher Wray's shops in the King's Road, London.

So much for glass. Of course I have done no more than tip my toes into the shallows of this vast and intriguing ocean, but many others more qualified than I am are around to steer you through the reefs, viz.

Books: *Antique Glass for Pleasure and Profit* by Geoffrey Wills (Gifford, 1971)

Collecting Glass by Norman W. Webber (David & Charles, 1972)

Glass Through the Ages by Barrington Haynes (Penguin, 1969)

Nailsea Glass by Keith Vincent (David & Charles, 1975)

Goss China

> *The self-same sun that shines upon his court*
> *Hides not his visage from our cottage.*
> *A Winter's Tale* by Shakespeare

Adolphus W. Goss of Stoke-on-Trent (son of William Henry Goss, founder of the Goss pottery works in 1858) was a man with an idea. It occurred to Adolphus, a keen student of heraldry, that small china artifacts printed with civic coats of arms might be just the souvenir that holidaymakers would like to take home with them. Overnight—almost—the mantels of Britain were cluttered with small ivory-glazed knick-knacks of no particular distinction.

You've all seen them. Tygs and ewers and urns and jugs, but what you may not know and ought to is that these things are collected and that according to the astonishing catalogue issued by George Vaughan of Lower Pitfold, Critchmere Lane, Haslemere, Surrey, not one of them is worth less than £2.

In fact these objects do less than justice to the skills of the Goss potters (William was a master modeller at Copelands). When they put themselves out, they could produce work of some sophistication, and it is the cottages, the architectural models and the busts

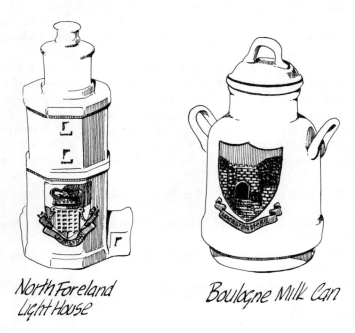

North Foreland Light House   Boulogne Milk Can

which command the best prices. For example Braunton Lighthouse (£125), John Bunyan's cottage, Elstow (£250), Christchurch Old Court House (£165) and the Hop Kiln, Kent (£500) give some indication of how far these Goss-hawks are prepared to go. *Any* Goss cottage is worth collecting and is worth at least £35, but study the models carefully before you buy them. Cracks, chips and faded crests diminish the value considerably. Hair-line cracks, invisible in a gloomy shop, may be self-evident in daylight. Mr Vaughan's prices are for pieces in pristine condition.

The cottages are particularly vulnerable to damage, and you should check (or require a guarantee from the vendor) that no restorative work has been carried out. Look extra carefully at the chimneys.

Izaac Walton's Cottage

The age of Goss models is of less importance but early ones are impressed W. H. Goss, while later ones display the Goshawk imprint with the firm's name. Any model with a military, naval, pictorial, or commemorative crest is particularly desirable, and so is a 'matching' crest (a Worcester crest on a Worcester jug for example).

Mr Vaughan conducts monthly postal auctions of Goss china and publishes *Collector's Gossip* relating to Goss and other crested china—because Goss was not left for long alone in his field; other potters emulated his success, and the output of some of them (Carlton, Arcadian and Shelley especially) is not to be despised.

In 1929 the Goss factory went bankrupt and was sold, yet Adolphus's brainwave continues to give pleasure and civic pride to all manner of people.

Books: *A Handbook of Goss China* by John Galpin (J. Galpin, 1972)

The Price Guide to the Models of W. H. Goss by Roland Ward (Antique Collectors Club)

Instruments

> *He made an instrument to know*
> *If the moon shine at full or no.*
> Samuel Butler

England is the place for scientific instruments: is and was. By the end of the eighteenth century glass-making had become sufficiently sophisticated for the large-scale production of scientific instruments, and no gentleman's home was complete without a globe, a telescope, and, as likely as not, a microscope. Now with the exception of professional scientists and C. P. Snow, few of us have any instruments in our house except radios, food mixers and hired television sets. Since Britain was a nation which depended upon its navy for survival and imperial expansion, the making of navigational aids was an honoured profession and reached a point of such excellence that art and science rejoiced together over octant and theodolite, orrery and globe. England is where the finest instruments are to be found. The Greenwich Maritime Museum (for naval artefacts), the Museum of the History of Science at Oxford and the Science Museum in London (for scientific instruments) are where you must go to study the finest and most beautiful examples in the world.

Then decide to specialise. David Weston of Curzon Street, W.1 who deals in such things, told me that he could teach me all there was to learn about sextants in an hour and a half, after which I could invest profitably and securely, for in four years the cost of a sextant has quadrupled from £30 to £120 (buying price). There is a sound reason for this increase. Since it is still cheaper to buy an antique instrument than to have a new one made (an old theodolite would cost £200 at auction, a new one would cost £400 in a shop) there is at present little danger of the forgers and fakers honing in.

Of course you still need to be wary. An old sundial which might cost £300 would be worth £400 if it boasted the signature of its maker. And consequently there are wicked men buying old sundials and adding new signatures to them. But you will not be taken in, because you will study the signature through a lens and discover that it has bright shining edges, which it would not have were it as old as it pretends to be.

So far as optical instruments are concerned I hesitate to state the obvious, but the most important thing to ensure is that they work. Chipped china, damaged silver, used stamps; these are all worth a reasonable percentage of their pristine value; but a microscope or telescope with a broken lens or a bit missing is almost valueless, since it is extremely difficult and vastly expensive to find anyone capable of replacing old precision parts.

The profit margins of dealers in scientific instruments are not great, ten or twenty per cent at most, and this is because the market is an international one. It is far easier to find a purchaser for a theodolite or a globe than for, say, a fine English watercolour, and, for this reason, most dealers will guarantee to buy back your purchase from you in a year's time at the same price, should you wish it. And this is not a guarantee that you are likely to obtain from a stamp collector, for instance, a picture dealer, or a greengrocer.

If such things at such prices alarm you, and your bank manager does not appreciate the sound investing principles which have led you to desire astrolabes and graphometers, you may settle for opera glasses, which are attractive, useful, readily available, and just beginning to interest the People with the Money. Some of them, particularly French ones and those in tortoiseshell and ivory and mother-of-pearl (I refer to the opera glasses and not the moneyed people) are particularly agreeable and come in velvet-lined cases. Check that you can see through them—then snap them up!

Books: *Scientific Instruments of the 17th and 18th Centuries and Their Makers* by Maurice Dumas (Batsford, 1972)
Collecting and Restoring Scientific Instruments by Roland Pearsall (David & Charles, 1974)

Ivory

At that age I was not squeamish about killing animals, but I had never shot an elephant and never wanted to. (Somehow it always seems worse to kill a large animal.) Besides, there was the beast's owner to be considered. Alive, the elephant was worth at least a hundred pounds; dead, he would only be worth the value of his tusks— five pounds, possibly.

'Shooting An Elephant' by George Orwell

The most important thing about ivory—and particularly where the elephant, walrus and hippo are concerned—is where it came from. The word ivory may, if you have a mind for such things, be traced all the way back through Egyptian (*ābu*) and Coptic (*ebou*) and Hebrew (*Shenhabbim*) to the Sanskrit word *ibhas*, and it was always related to the tusk of the elephant; but it's also used now to mean the tusk of the walrus and hippo. Tusk is harder than tooth and consequently more serviceable. (The very earliest ivory carvings were cut from the tusks of the mammoth some 20,000 years ago, but I just throw that in to confuse you—and to show off.) The elephant's tusk is of the first quality and the difference in price between elephant and walrus ivory is some thirty-five per cent, so how can you tell?

Elephant ivory is entirely smooth, but grained. Walrus ivory has a sort of translucent waxy appearance. It's hard and takes a fine polish, but lacks the fine grain of elephant tusk. The base of walrus ivory objects is often ornamented to conceal its origins. Bone is uneven in colour with black streaks and a circular grain like the grain in a tree trunk.

All of which is of some importance since the ivory market—and particularly the market in Japanese ivories—has seen a steady increase in prices over the last few years, a rise which has ignored all other trends. These ivories, usually *Netsuke* (pronounced 'netski'), the toggle on a Japanese gentleman's belt, and *Inro*, the seal secured by the toggle, have a curious history.

The great age for Japanese *Netsuke* was the early part of the nineteenth century, but the revolution in 1868 brought into fashion European costume, so that later ivories were made chiefly for the export market, and were consequently trashy and decadent. For the first half of this century they could be picked up in junk shops for a few pence (even the fine early ones) and when the post-war fashion for collecting got under way in earnest, *Netsuke* were ignored. But in the sixties the craze for *Netsuke* gained momentum. They are remarkable objects, homely and jocular rather than sublimely spiritual, sometimes erotic in a genial sort of way, or beautifully representative of the world of insects, birds and fishes. The Japanese have always liked things small (*haiku*, miniature trees, ladies' feet); their *Netsuke* and *Inro* exemplify this.

Not all of them are made of ivory—many other materials, including tortoiseshell, enamel and even dried mushroom, are employed —and of those which are, only some are signed. Since the prices of signed *Netsuke* are significantly higher than the rest, and since it has been known for signatures to be forged, you might do well to concentrate on unsigned examples. But study the overall aesthetics of the piece, the craftsmanship (the finer the detail the better), the functionalism (it should not have sharp edges lest its owner sit down too suddenly), the coloration and the patina. If you still like it, buy it, for it won't depreciate in value.

I have monitored prices from £35 for a crawling Chinaman (together with a silver-mounted Cairngorm), £52 for an octopus and a dog, £50 for a Jovial Chinaman with a water-gourd on his back, to £70 for a toad with insect on a lily. Naturally, exceptional signed examples fetch a lot more than this, over £2,000 the man from Sotheby's said, but such pieces are for the cognoscenti.

I should mention that less intricately carved and more modestly priced English ivories, card- and bodkin-cases, snuffboxes and combs, mirror-backs and hunting horns, Edwardian cocktail sticks and other ephemera and impedimenta are always available at auctions and on stalls at prices from £10–£25, and very nice too.

I'm also extremely happy to report that since 1976 it has no longer been permitted to import or export raw and unmade-up items of ivory and tortoiseshell. Besides protecting elephants and tortoises, this legislation will also protect collectors of ivory, since forgers will no longer be able to purchase the raw materials for their nefarious activities so cheaply. Prices of all ivory goods are bound to rise.

And, if you already own some nice ivory, and if it appears alarmingly yellow, don't, I beg you, try to clean it. Damp cotton wool won't hurt but anything more potent could be disastrous. The yellow is only a sign of old age, and, as with grannies, quite attractive.

Books: *Ivory* by O. Beigbeder (Weidenfeld and Nicolson, 1965)
      Collectors' Netsuke by Raymond Bushell (Weatherhill, 1972)

Jade

> *Virtue is like a rich stone, best plain set.*
> *Essays*, 'Of Beauty' by Francis Bacon

I once interviewed Arthur Negus at his home in Cheltenham. I was anxious lest I might be too garrulous (a cardinal sin in interviewers) or too shy, and took along with me a little snuff bottle from the stall to jolly things along if they got sticky—they didn't. The man was ebullient and helpful, but before I left I brought out my bottle and asked him whether he thought it was jade.

'Soon tell,' he said. 'Can I scratch it with a knife?' He tried, ruined the knife. 'No. Well, if it'll cut glass, it's probably jade.' He put it to the window pane, described a wide arc with his arm. His wife brought in the tea-things, saw what he was up to. 'Oh, you're not cutting up the window *again!*'

'Never mind, dear, I'll make it into a beautiful flower for you.'

(It wasn't jade, however. The man at the Victoria and Albert looked down his nose at it, and when men at the V. and A. look down their noses, you know that nothing will ever be the same again, indeed that nothing ever was.) Negus, of course, was right about jade; it is hard enough to cut glass, though not as hard as many other stones such as topaz, corundum, and diamond, which will cut anything, even the hard heart of a movie queen.

But jade is not just hard, it is . . . *weird*. It feels cold to the touch, but requires to be fondled. It is sympathetic. Confucius allowed it to have charity in its lustre, honesty in its translucency, wisdom in the purity of its ring, courage in its brittleness and impartiality in that, although it has sharp edges, it injures nobody. The Chinese character for jade is the same as for nobility.

There are two principle kinds of jade, nephrite, a silicate of calcium and magnesium, and jadeite, a silicate of sodium and aluminium. The oldest Chinese jades are nephrite (of which the most desirable is the seed-jade), and although most of these are shaded in different tints of green, creams, yellows and greys are also found, as is the much admired 'mutton-fat' nephrite. Nephrite is more opaque than jadeite, not quite so hard, oily to the touch, more demanding of the craftsman. Jadeite is glassy, translucent, in various shades of green, mauve and white.

Other hardstones are sometimes optimistically mistaken for jade, as is soapstone, which is not very hard at all, and much easier to come by—though less easy to sell—than jade.

To understand jade thoroughly, it is necessary to immerse yourself in Chinese history, to embrace the Taoist mythology, to come to terms with *yin* and *yang*. I have done none of these things, and have to confess that I find Fabergé's use of nephrite and associated stones to carve miraculously life-like sprays of flowers and fruit and animals more remarkable than the mystical masterpieces of the Chinese craftsmen.

The finest jade is to be found where the finest jazz and pizza are: in New York City, at the Metropolitan Museum. The sort of jade I find at local auctions is priced between £14 for a small medallion to £55 for a tiny pair of *kylins* but this is a uniquely specialised field (a Ch'ien Lung bowl could set you back £4,000), and fools should not rush in where mandarins fear to tread.

Books: *Jade* by J. P. Palmer (Spring Books, 1968)
     Jade by Geoffrey Wills (Mayflower, 1970)

Jewellery

As a jewel of gold in a swine's snout, so is a fair woman which is without discretion.

Proverbs

'The trouble with this country,' said the Bond Street jeweller, 'is that there are too many consciences. Money's become a dirty word, and it shouldn't be. What we need is a rapid shift to the right.' He was called away to take a telephone call. 'Oh, another thousand won't make any difference,' I heard him say. His cousin asked me my views, and I explained that those who do the dirty jobs should get the most money.

'The people who clean the dead bodies at the mortuaries get a lot of money,' he said, 'but that's a really dirty job, the worst.'

Gold and silver beamed down on us from display cabinets. My battered old Post Office van was appallingly conspicuous on Bond Street's neat yellow lines. I tried not to think about washing dead bodies. 'Tell me about bargains . . .' I said.

They said that you didn't want to buy modern jewellery and have to pay VAT. They said that a nice piece of antique jewellery was an excellent investment, but if you wanted to be sure, you should buy it from a good dealer's—'us or Cartier's', they said. It's true that at a large dealer's you will have to pay a little more, but you get the guarantee of their reputation, and that's better than going just anywhere, isn't it? Of course, they said, if you *have* the knowledge, you can go round the markets and buy from the know-nothings, but I could tell that they thought that I *didn't* have the knowledge (they're right) and that anyone who read a book written by me would be unlikely to have it either.

But anyway I must pass on to you some tips for recognizing treasures should you chance to find them by one of the methods described earlier in this invaluable book.

Pearls

There is no way you can be 100% certain of differentiating between cultured pearls and the real things. If the pearls are *very* irregular they wouldn't be real, but then they wouldn't be cultured either so that's not much use.

Diamonds

First of all, will the diamond cut glass? If it won't—and if the attempt leaves rub-marks—it can't be a diamond. If it will, it probably is. Should the setting be very elaborate, that may mean that it's a diamond, or it may just mean that the cultured people who made it wanted you to think so.

Gold Pendant

Cameo Brooch

Pearl Covered Victorian Pendant

Star Diamond on Blue Enamel

French Pearl c1920

Rubies and Coloured Diamonds

These are the cream of the cream. If you find these in your job lot you might even be able to afford a season ticket on the railways.

But for these, as for pearls and white diamonds, the only way to be certain is to send them to the Chamber of Commerce who, for a modest *pourboire*, will test them for you.

Gold
Since gold has only been hallmarked since the turn of the century, any reasonably old piece will be open to doubt. You can usually tell whether something is gold by looking at it, but to be sure, and to confirm just how pure the gold is, you need a touchstone and acids of various strengths obtainable at your chemist.

Rub a bit of the 'gold' off on to the touchstone and apply the acid test. Nine-carat gold will fade in a weak solution, 18-carat (three-quarters pure) will need a stronger one, and 24-carat, or pure gold, will fade only in a powerful acid. To price your piece of gold you then need to multiply the weight of the article by the price of gold on the commodity market, and, if it's 18-carat subtract one quarter, or, if it's 9-carat, subtract three-eighths of the price. Obviously this price is the scrap price, so you should add a bit for age and workmanship and interest and sentiment.

Mind you, there's plenty of fun to be had out of costume jewellery, especially since you may find in 'a jewel-box and contents' a nice piece of art nouveau or deco or anything. I always display a jewel-box on my stall. Customers who are children at heart can never resist a lucky dip.

Books: *Investing in Antique Jewellery* by Richard Falkine (Corgi, 1971)
Victorian Jewellery by Deirdre O'Day (Charles Letts—Collectors Guides, 1974)
Victorian Jewellery by Margaret Flower (Cassell, 1967)

Medals

The English infantry, in close fighting, is the very devil.
General Foy at Waterloo
I have them there at last, those English!
Napoleon at Waterloo

Service Medals
What the medal collector very often gets that neither the philatelist nor the numismatist gets is the recipient's name, rank and regiment

or ship on the edge of the medal. Furthermore, if the recipient was an officer, the service records will enable you to build up a complete dossier on him.

The campaign medal was first issued in 1815 as a result of Waterloo. In 1848 Queen Victoria instituted the Military General Service Medal, which was backdated so that it applied to all battles from 1793. However, long before these official medals, there had been a history of privately issued ones.

The first award for courage was the medal given to Sir Robert Welch in 1642 for rescuing the standard at Edge Hill, although most of the early awards were for naval encounters. Hence the 'Ark in Flood' medal which Queen Elizabeth gave to the admirals and commanders who fought the Spanish Armada. These medals were gold and silver and could be worn around the neck. But Drake's medal, personally awarded to him, is a cameo cut in onyx, set with diamonds and rubies, attributed to Vincinteno. On the reverse is the date (1575) and a miniature by Nicholas Hilliard.

The Waterloo medal might be a good starter for new collectors; but it will cost you rather more than £175. Be suspicious of buying medals with several bars (which technically makes them more attractive to the cognoscenti). It has been known for charlatans to contrive a medal with lots of bars, the bars coming from other sources. The proper number of bars to any one medal may be verified in the army or navy rolls.

Prices of service medals are high and, though in the course of collecting you will gain fascinating insights into social, military and political history, I should not recommend service medals as ideal for non-specialist collectors of limited means. If you happen upon an interesting medal you will not be hard pressed to find a home for it at Spinks, Stanley Gibbons, Haywards or other specialist dealers.

Commemorative Medals

The Battle of Britain, the defeat of the Armada, and the nine hundredth anniversary of Westminster Abbey have all been celebrated by the striking of a commemorative medal. More curiously, a medal was struck in 1809 to express the outraged feelings of London theatre-goers when Kemble had the gall to raise seat prices in order to pay for his new folly, the Theatre Royal, Covent Garden. Not only have there been some notable medals, there have been some exceptionally gifted medallists, including Antonio Pisano, known as Pisanello of Verona (*c.* 1395–1455) who was the equivalent of Donatello in sculpture, and Benvenuto Cellini. If, however, you happen upon a Pisanello or a Cellini, I suggest you take expert advice before rushing out to buy a Vermeer or a racehorse or a stamp to post a letter; they are much forged.

The Victoria Cross

Recently there has been a sudden flurry of limited edition medallions; the manufacturers tend to take full page advertisements in the colour supplements, and leave you feeling like a fool and a Philistine and a social reject should you resist their blandishments. However you might do well to do so. Unless these limited editions have unusual aesthetic qualities—they seldom have—they are unlikely to prove a good investment. And the other rule for the wide-eyed ingénue stepping into this world of urbane sophisticates is: specialise. As with so many areas of collecting empiricism is an expensive indulgence.

Books: *Collecting Medals and Decorations* by Alec A. Purves (Seaby, 1971)

Collecting Military Medals: A Beginners' Guide by Colin Norbeth (Lutterworth, 1971)

Model Furniture

> *My life has crept so long on a broken wing*
> *Thro' cells of madness, haunts of horror and fear,*
> *That I come to be grateful at last for a little thing.*
> 'Maud' by Alfred, Lord Tennyson

A publisher of my acquaintance, an eccentric in whose company one is always liable to have adventures, has adopted as his motto 'Small is Beautiful'. He collects telescopes. I don't think he is aware of the paradox.

But for people who live in bedsitters and would like to collect antique furniture the motto would do very nicely—they should collect model furniture, which is also called miniature furniture. It is *also* called doll's house furniture, but quite incorrectly, because doll's house furniture was made specifically for doll's houses, whereas the slightly larger model furniture—and here we run up against another difficulty. What exactly was model furniture *for*?

Perhaps it was not *for* anything. Perhaps it was just for ornament, a thing of beauty and a toy forever. Some say that model furniture was made as an apprentice's passing-out test. Which is obviously silly, although many still believe it. Why should an apprentice need a test at all? And why should his master waste his time and materials on something evidently useless? It is far more likely that pieces of model furniture were made for window display or as travellers' samples; after all they could hardly hump a full-sized chest of drawers from door to door.

But whatever they were for, these things are delightful and sit as prettily on a stall as they would on a drawing-room table. Fine examples may incidentally be studied at the Bethnal Green Museum. Some of them have sailors' love knots carved on them, indicating perhaps that they were carved, as scrimshaw work on whales' teeth was, by sailors on their long absences from their girls; others less crude are perfect copies of classic designs. Of course it was not always possible for them to be *absolutely* perfect scale models—particularly so with doll's house furniture—as the wood

Miniature Furniture

wouldn't stand it, and some refinements, such as lapped dovetailing on the drawers, had to be sacrificed. Brass handles and escutcheons tended to be larger than they should have been, as did the marquetry work, but the skills in the making of these little pieces are self-evident. Reproductions abound—check the wood of the drawers in the little chests; it's sometimes very modern-looking—but prices remain reasonable (from about £15 for a miniature chest). Models are often sold in specialist toy auctions.

Books: *Collecting Miniature Antiques* by G. B. and T. Hughes
       (Heinemann, 1973)
       Miniature Antiques by Jean Lathain (Black, 1974)

Model Soldiers

From my point of view, you are not surrounded—your opponent is surrounded. Act accordingly.

Moshe Dayan

As I write this, wars are going on in many parts of the world, with soldiers and sailors the playing pieces of an intricate game of political manoeuvring. Which leads one to wonder, couldn't they do it all with models? And if so, why don't they? Or do they? Is there at this moment in a lead-lined bunker deep down inside a mountain in neutral territory a group of men from Washington, from Moscow and from Peking pushing model soldiers around a map of the world to decide who shall run the show for the next hundred years? I bet there is. The Goon Show anticipated the situation. They had Churchill tow a cardboard model of the British Isles into the Atlantic to fool the Germans; but those swine responded by bombing it with cardboard bombs!

The very earliest model soldiers were made in southern Germany. They were quite large, the horses and knights being cast in solid bronze, gilded and enamelled, while the soldiers were made of slate. Tin and lead alloys replaced bronze and slate and by the eighteenth and nineteenth centuries the toymakers of Nuremberg had modelled most of the soldiery of Europe, and quite a few of the civilians and their animals too.

All these models were 'flats', that is to say two-dimensional figures on small stands. They varied considerably in size until Heinrichsen standardised the models to the 30mm 'Nuremberg scale'. The flats were followed by 'semi-flats' in low relief and the French developed *'rond bosse'* or 'solid' figures in the 1870s. To-

Britain's Hollow-Cast Soldiers 45mm

wards the end of the century William Brittain produced the first hollow-cast three-dimensional figures. Being both more realistic than the German models and cheaper (containing less metal) they captured the market. Brittain expanded rapidly and by the outbreak of the Second World War he could supply every regiment in the British army.

Since the war the application of plastic has kept prices down and enabled the manufacturers to retain excellent detail, but there is little pleasure in handling plastic as opposed to tin and lead soldiers.

Early British models have round bases in place of the Continental square ones, and are highly prized, especially in sets; some of the connoisseur pieces made by men like Roger Benoud and Robert Courtenay of Slough sell for above £50. Many of the models made by contemporary artists are supplied unpainted if requested.

Books: *Model Soldiers* by Massimo Alberini (fine illustrations— Orbis Books, 1972)
Model Soldiers by Henry Harris (Octopus Books, 1972)

Paperweights

> *Anything may happen in France.*
> Duc de la Rochefoucauld

It happens as if by magic. Some unassuming artefact is included in an intangible New Year's Honour's list and becomes almost overnight an antique, a desirable object, a collector's item, expensive.

In order for it to happen, certain conditions need to be present. The artefact needs to have some intrinsic desirability (not much, *vide* Goss China, but some). It should be both rare enough to be hard to get and yet not so rare as to discourage collectors. It should be identifiable and dateable and have romantic anecdotes attaching to it. It should have at least one rich and notorious patron.

Paperweights fulfilled all these requirements. The rich and notorious patron was King Farouk who, perhaps because the technique of millefiori (literally, 'a thousand flowers') was practised in ancient Egypt, cornered the market in the 1950s and bought up all the very best examples which he and his heavies could lay their hands upon. These paperweights were, without question, desirable, and the best of them were both rare and identifiable.

It was the glassworkers on the island of Murano near Venice who adapted the Egyptian technique of millefiori to paperweights at the time of the Renaissance. They kept at it (and still do) producing patterns of dancers and animals and flowers until Pierre Biglagia joined in and had the temerity to display his work at the Exhibition of Austrian Industry in May 1845. The French were particularly intrigued and Pierre showed them how. From 1845 to 1850 at Baccarat and St Louis (in the Vosges) and at Clichy where Henry Miller was to introduce *his* techniques to the French some hundred years later, the superb French paperweights, which now command such large sums, were produced. They were not the main business of the factories, but a profitable sideline. Ironically, it was not the

Baccarat Close Millefiori Weight

millefiori patterns (bundles of glass cones in different colour combinations forming intricate designs) which proved the most remarkable of the French paperweights. The bouquets of flowers, the mushrooms, the birds and insects, the salamanders and fruit and vegetables (mainly from St Louis) and above all the accurate representations of flowers are what King Farouk and latterly other crowned heads and monogrammed shirts pay such fortunes for.

Because we are talking in thousands of pounds (£6,000 in 1968 for a St Louis salamander, £5,200 for a Clichy convolvulus, £2,050 for a Baccarat butterfly and primrose), not hundreds. And yet before the first war these were sold for shillings and before the second for less than £10.

Now I do not expect you to pay thousands of pounds for a paperweight and you would be rash to do so, since there are a number of convincing fakes on the market. But you might care to turn your attention to the home manufactured, native born paperweight. At the same time as Biglagia was instructing the French, our own glass tax was being removed so that some Clichy craftsmen were able to travel to Stourbridge and practise there. But we had already developed our own green bottle-glass varieties (often thought to be door-stops and not paperweights) and the later Victorians and Edwardians produced paperweights with heavy clear glass covering circular seaside engravings and prints. These have a modest charm and can easily be acquired at around £2–£3 while modern and reproduction millefiori designs are over £25. A word too about the paperweights made from Cornish serpentine rock which are still being sold as souvenirs in Cornish shops. These are both cheap and agreeable and are surely the stuff that future collections are made of.

Recently the Whitefriars Glass Company began producing limited editions of paperweights in old millefiori styles. These are attractive pieces in their own right as are the products of the Perthshire Works. But all are much lighter in the hand than the great French originals; they sell at between £50 and £100.

And, by the way, if you think you have a St Louis forget-me-not or a Clichy Latticinio bouquet go and call on Patricia McCawley at Spink's. She'll know.

Books: *Glass Paperweights* by J. Mackay (Ward Lock, 1973)
      Antique Glass Paperweights from France by P. K. McCawley (Spink & Son, 1968)

Papier-Mâché

It is to be noted that when any part of this paper appears dull, there is a design in it.

                    Sir Richard Steele in *The Tatler*

Henry Clay was the man, Birmingham the place and 1772 the year by whom and in which papier-mâché was first patented in England. It came to us from Persia where it was used for picture frames.

Originally it was composed of paper pulp stiffened with glue, chalk, plaster, sand, sizing and gum mastic. It would be subjected to great heat, then allowed to cool. Another layer of paper and the process would be repeated until there was sufficient thickness and strength. Then you could paint and varnish. Being heat- and damp-resistant it seemed just the job for moulded cornices and ceilings, but to Henry Clay it had other uses . . . So did it too to the Marks and Spencer of papier-mâché, Jennens and Bettridge, also of Birmingham, who extended Clay's ideas and dominated the world market during the early part of the nineteenth century.

In their hands papier-mâché became all things to all men, a magical substance from which you could fashion trays, music racks, screens, chairs, workboxes, teapoys, writing cases, inkwells, vases, tables, cabinets, coasters, fans, pen trays, letter racks, blotters, canterburys, pole-screens and beds—but with a substructure, thank goodness, of iron.

Most papier-mâché has painted decoration against a black ground, and is inlaid with mother-of-pearl or Nautilus shell, and either decorated with sprays of flowers or japanned.

Papier Mâché Work Box & Writing Case
Both Inlaid with Mother of Pearl

Frequently you will find to your disgust that your agreeable purchase is badly damaged—chunks may even be missing. Fortunately one of the joys of papier-mâché is that it is simple to repair. You will remember the technique from your kindergarten or primary school. You tear newspaper into scraps, soak it in water for a day, strain off the surplus, and mix the remaining pulp with flour paste. Then with a strong adhesive you are ready to decorate. Alternatively, and if you have less time to spare, you may plug the gap with plastic wood, and blacken it with blackboard black or stove black.

I cannot but think that Victorian and Georgian papier-mâché is one of the most exciting bargains around. Prices are still low. At a country house auction a nineteenth-century dish by Jennens and Bettridge which was decorated with a pleasantly ruined abbey fetched a desultory £24. But prices of papier-mâché depend so greatly upon condition and execution that it's difficult to suggest prices. An unsigned tray will cost between £25 and £30, a good-quality landscaped Jennens and Bettridge tray perhaps £100.

Papier-mâché is usable, repairable, and still quite cheap. What more can one ask of anything (or anyone)? Snap it up before it's too late.

Book: *English Papier-Mâché of the Georgian and Victorian Periods* by Shirley Spaulding De Voe (Barrie & Jenkins, 1971)

Pewter

> *The end is easily foretold*
> *When every blessed thing you hold*
> *Is made of silver or of gold—*
> *You long for simple pewter.*
> > *The Gondoliers* by W. S. Gilbert

You may long for it, but simple it isn't. I read books about pewter and strange reading they made. There were the Cornish tin mines in which only a Spartacus might expect to survive. There were apprentices flogged and pewterers dishonoured. In the New World there was the wife of the President loading her covered wagon with all her plate and pewter and setting off for the Bank of Maryland pursued by the advancing British. Indeed it's a wonder that 'the story of pewter' has not been filmed with Charlton Heston (hammered around the rim but with genuine touch marks) in the title role.

The trouble with pewter, which I regard as rivalling silver at its elegant and unostentatious best is that
—nobody has ever agreed upon what it is
—nobody has ever regularized the system of touch marks, so that the forging of pewter is perfectly legal
—many genuine pieces were never marked
—it is malleable and it is a great deal easier to reproduce a convincing copy of a great original than to do the same for a picture, say, or a piece of furniture.

Touchmarks

Fly + Thompson
London
1737-1745

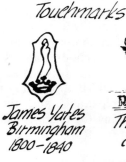

James Yates
Birmingham
1800-1840

RODWELL
Thomas Rodwell
c1704-1730

John Letha
Edinburg
1718-17

What is pewter? It's an alloy with tin as its main constituent and one or more of the following: lead, antimony, copper, bismuth. H. J. L. J. Massé, who did for pewter what the Beatles did for Liverpool, sorted pewter into thirteen different grades, but received little credit for his industry since each grade was worth much the same. Many people confused pewter with Britannia metal, which is a poor relation; you couldn't blame them since early examples are indistinguishable. Later on Britannia metal deteriorated in quality, though quantities of it were used in Art Nouveau pewter, and inferior modern stuff. As John Bright put it:

> *Silence is golden,*
> *Speech is silvern,*
> *But to say one thing*
> *And mean another is*
> *Britannia Metal.*

The only hint which I can give you is that to my eyes there is more moonlight in pewter, and more sunlight in Britannia metal.

So far as the silver content of pewter is concerned, it's a case of the silver being in the tin 'not because anyone put it there, but because nobody could get it out'.

Pewter was used for almost any purpose you could mention, and for some purposes I hope you will not mention. It was to be found in church and hospital, tavern and domestic kitchen. In the eighteenth century and thereafter china plate ousted pewter plates from the dinner table, while silver, Sheffield plate and electro-plate took over the table adornments. The consequence was that the Victorians (*vide* W. S. Gilbert *super*) tended to disregard pewter. Well, most of them did. William Smith and Charles Eaton, an ingenious but illiterate pair of mudlarks from the banks of the Thames, produced naive pseudo-medieval items, which got past even the Pewter Society—and getting past them was like getting past Horatius on his bridge—and which are now collected in their own right. Well so they should be, these Billies and Charlies as they are called, because after all they are not fakes in the sense that they were the original products of skilled though untrained talents. The intention was to defraud, but the results delight.

Single Reed Plate   Triple Reed Plate

Now let us suppose that you acquire a piece of pewter, an old porringer perhaps. You got it cheap, because it's not only corroded but damaged, so what to do? Soak it in paraffin for a while and you will remove most of the oxidisation.

Boil and soak it all night in washing soda and some of the corrosion may go, but don't use abrasives, and *never* dip pewter in acid. Part of the charm of pewter is in its dents, although these may be removed if you choose to do so by the use of a horn-headed hammer, resting the article on a sandbag. If you have a valuable piece you should send it to a specialist.

You may acquire some of the Liberty range of Tudric ware, with strong Celtic influence (£25 or thereabouts for a small vase), or you may go for the grand things such as chalices. But I would recommend that you concentrate on the uncomplicated things which pewter did so successfully, like plates and mugs and measures. And since it will take you months of book-study or evening classes before you begin to recognise even rudimentary forgeries, I suggest you leave the Big Time to the Big Boys. You meddle with them at your peril.

Prices vary enormously but an antique tankard might be around £15, a plate around £12, a pair of antique peppers £18 and a pair of old candlesticks between £40 and £50. All glass-bottomed tankards are comparatively modern, and for these £3 is the going rate.

Books: *Pewter: A Guide for Collectors* by Kenneth Ulyett (Muller, 1973)

English Pewter Touch Marks by Radway Jackson (Foulsham, 1970)

Antique Pewter of the British Isles by Ronald Michaelis (Dover, 1972)

The Pewter Collector by H. J. L. J. Massé, revised by Michaelis (Barrie & Jenkins, 1971)

Photographs

From today painting is dead.
Paul Delaroche, painter, on seeing his first daguerreotype

One hundred and fifty years they've been at it, not that long, and yet they've produced films, television, X-rays, microphotography, press photography, photographs by satellite and photographs of distant constellations. Cameras invade the human body, snapping away busily like tourists ('Here we have the spleen and here . . .') and spy out the mummified remains of Egyptian princesses. Perhaps when we conquer time we'll even be able to photograph the future.

It all began in 1826 with Joseph Nicéphore Niépce taking a 'Heliograph' of the view from his attic window near Gras on an eight-hour exposure. A colleague of Niépce, Louis Daguerre, produced his first successful daguerreotype in the year Victoria came to the throne (1837); this was two years after William Fox Talbot made his first 'Calotype' by a negative/positive process, which enabled him to print on paper and make copies. New processes and improvements continued apace. David Octavius Hill and Robert Adamson took a composite photograph of a convention of Scottish protestants—it measured five feet by twelve feet and kept the pair occupied for twenty-three years. Was it worth it? Nobody said.

For an impressive list of all the most important Victorian photographers I must refer you to Peter Castle's excellent and attractive book *Collecting and Valuing Old Photographs*. But mention should be made of Roger Fenton's set of 360 photographs of the Crimean War, of Paul Martin's magnificent candid snaps of the workers at home, at work, and at the seaside, of Lewis Carroll's portraits of

E J Marley Jumping Man c 1884

little girls, including one of the original Alice, and of course, of Julia Margaret Cameron, the outstanding figure in Victorian photography. In the summer of 1974 prices for Mrs Cameron's slightly sentimental but affecting portraits trebled and quadrupled, as did the prices of other old photographs, but they have steadied since. Probably you will now find better bargains in the less

143

trampled paths of photographic equipment and the works of unknown and amateur photographers, whose unattributed work can frequently be found selling for a pound or two at provincial salerooms and in antique shops. Anything at all unusual or historic is popular, and 'lucky' photographs of Emily Davison throwing herself under the King's horse during the 1913 Derby or Winston Churchill at the Siege of Sidney Street would be thought *most* desirable. Look out too for Muybridge's semi-nude studies of 'Animal Locomotion'—there is a collection of these at Kingston Public Library—and for those early nude studies 'for artists only', which gave rise to a sudden burst of artistic energy the length and breadth of the country.

You should also learn to distinguish between the daguerreotype with its bright reflective surface, the ambrotype, which has a greyish appearance and which, though tinted or hand-coloured, is rarely signed, and the ferrotype, or tintype, which has a black appearance and metallic finish.

Or you could collect stereoscopic viewers and cards (about £10), or old albums at about the same price. The scrap albums of the 1840s and 1850s were the forerunners of the early photograph albums whose photographs were haphazardly mounted with none of the 'production' that later Victorians were to add to their souvenir books. These albums are fascinating memorials to Victorian family life and all it stood for, and, if the faces seem gloomy and unsmiling, that may be because it was so difficult to

Victorian Photograph Album

hold a pose (as you would have been required to) for several minutes. Some of the albums are most artistic, with hand-painted border illustrations, silver clasps, ivory motifs, gold-edged pages, lacquer and so forth. Some of the albums included, as well as photographs and scraps, pressed flowers, menu cards, dance cards and theatre programmes. What could be nicer?

Where modern photographers are concerned, there are experts happily paying a thousand dollars for the works of artists like Irving Penn, although there is bound to be the considerable risk with photographers who are still alive that they may ruin everything by issuing more prints of the portrait you have just bought. Be properly suspicious of limited editions (which may just be a sly way of raising the price) and, as always, pay no more than you can afford for only those things which you really like.

Books: *Early Photographs and Early Photographers* by Oliver Matthews (Reedminster, 1973)

The History of Photography by Bennet Newhall (Secker & Warburg, 1972)

Collecting and Valuing Old Photographs by Peter Castle (Garnstone Press, 1973)

Victorian Photographs of Famous Men and Fair Women by Julia Margaret Cameron (Hogarth Press, 1973)

Pictures, Prints and Frames

> *When Sir Joshua Reynolds died*
> *All nature was degraded;*
> *The King dropped a tear in the Queen's ear*
> *And all his pictures faded.*
> 'On Art and Artists' by William Blake

You must understand my euphoria. I think I've just bought an Augustus John for £6. There he was, leaning against the back of an arm chair, a rather soppy pencil sketch of a plump lady with three naked children standing in a field and looking as though she would rather be back in Kensington. It is signed characteristically 'John' and, over-obviously I thought, it says Augustus John in great big letters on the back. All the catalogue said was: 'Pencil sketch framed and glazed'. So I bid for it and got it without much trouble and will pop it into the V & A for a professional opinion.

I tell this story as an illustration that at auctions anything may happen. And particularly so when pictures are sold as part of a general auction and the picture dealers are otherwise engaged.

It's a freakish world. I've been to exhibitions by local artists which form the centrepiece of some festival or other. The subjects of the pictures are predictable, the execution for the most part feeble and at best competent, and yet these same pictures are priced at a minimum of £30. (For a satirical view of such exhibitions you should read that brilliantly witty novel *The Guru and the Golf Club*, in which the first prize goes to the police poster warning against the Colorado Beetle!) Freakish, I'll say. For £22 I've bought a large maple-framed late eighteenth-century coloured glass engraving of an early and primitive steam omnibus—full of charm and atmosphere. For £20 you can buy delightful Victorian landscapes in oils and watercolours; while handsome ones can still be snapped up for even less. At a recent Buckell and Ballard auction a set of four contemporary prints by the brilliant Gerald Scarfe were sold for £31—a safer investment than a Building Society. And at any general auction it is possible to pick up cheap lots of pictures and prints. I recently paid £18 for twenty-six various prints and pictures at Phillips, Marylebone, and they contained: Item: One oval-shaped print in ditto frame after Cypriani and signed Mary Galloway 1793. Sold by me for a fiver. Item: Half a dozen original 1920s oils by one John Roulet. One of them shows Field Marshal Foch (looking not unlike a Bacon Pope) riding into a deserted and liberated Paris on a horse. I'm not parting with *that*. Item: A pair of coloured Morland prints. Sold by me for £4. Item: A Japanese silk-weave picture in a maple frame. Sold by me for £6—and so on. I apologize if I seem to be boasting; I try to forget my disasters!

Oils and watercolours are more straightforward than prints, which need some paragraphs of explanation. So, if technical things bore you, or you already know about printing processes, skip the next page or so.

There are three main categories of prints: relief, intaglio and planographic. These names suggest the different techniques involved. **Relief** implies *woodcuts*, extensively used in early book illustrations since the wood-block married well with the moveable type. **Intaglio** is the genus of which *engraving*, *mezzotint*, *aquatint* and *etching* are species. An engraver used his graver to plough runnels in the plate, creating the lines in his design. By 'cross-hatching' he could supply shading and texture. *Drypoint* engraving

Woodcut by Thomas Bewick (1753 - 1828)

used a pointed steel tool instead of a graver, and thus produced a freer line. William Rogers was the daddy of engravers in the late sixteenth century, and later artists discovered that there was money to be made from engraving, so that Hogarth deliberately coarsened his pictures when engraving to increase their popular appeal. William Woollet (1735–1785) made charming engravings from Stubbs's horses and Richard Wilson's landscapes, and Blake used the technique to illustrate his apocalyptic fantasies.

In the *mezzotint* the line was abolished altogether and the design was transferred on to a roughened copper plate. The mezzotint was an arduous undertaking but John Raphael Smith used it successfully on the works of Reynolds and Romney, and David Lucas applied it to Constable.

Etching, introduced to England in the seventeenth century, involves a plate being covered with a waxy composition and blackened in smoke. Thereafter the design is traced in reverse with etching needles laying bare the surface of the copper. Exposure to acid for varying lengths of time eats away the exposed metal to produce the picture.

The *aquatint* is a combination of mezzotint and etching but, where the mezzotint produces the effect of an oil painting, an aquatint is closer to a watercolour. Paul Sandby is the first great name in aquatinting. William and Thomas Daniell did fine topo-graphical work and H. T. Alken's sporting prints and Gillray's and Rowlandson's cartoons are aquatints.

In *lithography*, a process which came to England at the beginning of the nineteenth century, the print is flat (**planographic**). The draw-ing is made directly on to a stone or metal plate or transferred thence with a transfer paper in ink which has soap or tallow in it. The stone absorbs the grease, after which nitric acid is applied. The virtue of lithography is that it is your actual drawing and betrays (or doesn't betray) the artist's hand. Early prints were often hand-coloured, but by the 1840s colour lithography was introduced. Chromolithography permitted much copying of early masters.

As a general rule a good dark print implies that it was nice and 'early'; later impressions becoming faint and shadowy. On the bot-tom margin of a print you will find puzzling abbreviations. These need not puzzle and can be decoded thus:

delin.—drew

exc. or *exud.*—printed or published

f. or *fec.*—etched or engraved

figuravit—drew

inv.—designed

pinx.—painted

sc. or *sculp.*—engraved

When buying pictures, never back age against quality. Check the back of the frame and be suspicious if an old picture has been recently reframed. Remember that an old carved wood frame is worth a lot of money and a maple or rosewood frame can always be sold to a dealer regardless of what it frames.

There was a recent fashion for buying Louis Wain's whimsical cats—the market was flooded and a lot of Louis Wains were found to be forgeries. Currently Arthur Rackhams (all those pubescent fairies) are coming under suspicion. Watercolours have been a weak market in the last few years and together with etchings these are now much undervalued. David Routledge of Sotheby's told me that an investment of £20 in a good quality watercolour or £50 in a work by a major artist could not go wrong. I doubt whether you even need to spend as much as this. So far as subjects are con-cerned, pretty girls are always popular (surprise, surprise), but por-traits are less popular than landscapes. So the watercolour you want to hunt for is a nineteenth-century landscape, either un-attributed or signed by an accredited artist.

Glass paintings are still cheap and are usually attractively framed. Primitives, for which there was such a vogue ten years ago, are out of favour (which means that now is the time to buy them). And original cartoons are still absurdly cheap. Nor do I just mean the works of Phil May, Charles Keane, Spy, Low, Ernest Shepherd and other artists whose skills are evident on the pages of old volumes of *Punch*. Twentieth-century cartoonists should not be ignored.

Above all—and this applies to paintings and prints of every kind of pedigree—buy what you like. So you may have been foolish; it may be worthless, a forgery, a cheap copy, but if it cost you less than a fiver and gives you permanent pleasure it must be both cheaper and more satisfying than looking at television. Mustn't it?

Books: *Dictionary and Price Guide to English Watercolours 1750–1900* by D. Thomas and I. Bennett (Antique Collector's Club, 1970)
Victorian Painters by J. Mass (Barrie & Jenkins, 1969)
The Pelican History of Art edited by N. Pevsner (various volumes)
Etchings and Engravings by Walter Chamberlain (Thames and Hudson, 1973)
Prints for the Collector by Therle Hughes (Collectors Library, 1971)
Collecting English Watercolours by Derek Clifford (Baker, 1970)

Playing Cards

If you play let not a covetous desire to win another's money engage you to the losing your own; which will not only disturb your mind, but by the disreputation of being a Gamester, if you lose not your estate, you will certainly lose your credit and good name, than which there is nothing more valuable.

The Compleat Gamester, 1674

Little did I think, when Nicolas Norton sat one end of the pram and I the other, with the cards dealt out between us, that we were dealing in magic and divination. But now, thanks to Mr Stewart Culin of the Brooklyn Museum, I know that playing cards—and chess—derive from the divinatory use of the arrow and the classification of all things according to the Four Directions.

The earliest cards were Chinese, and were imitated from the Chinese paper notes in the Tang Dynasty (618–908 A.D.); these cards were both what you played *with* and what you played *for*. Then came the packs of 120 cards in three suits, coins, strings of coins and myriads of strings of coins, with three extra cards, the red flower, the white flower and the old thousand.

The earliest European cards were French, and Etienne Vignoles, known as Lahire, who invented the game of Piquet, also invented the four suit signs which replaced the Tarots and have been used in France ever since, *coeurs* (for the Church), *carreaux* (arrowheads or diamonds, representing the vassal class from whom the archers were recruited), *trèfles* or clover (clubs—the husbandmen) and *piques* (the points of lances or spades representing the knights themselves). Thus the old chess-based war-games became courtly games of chivalry. In 1440 came the first named court cards. For the knaves (*valets* in French) four famous knights, Lancelot, Hogier, Rolant and Valéry (later Hector), for the Queens, Rachel, Argine, Pallas and Judith, and for the Kings, Alexander, Caesar, Charlemagne and David.

As you might expect, the revolutionaries deposed the court cards when they disposed of the court and, until 1813, when the pre-Revolutionary cards were reinstated, the French played with Philosophers, Emblematic Personages and *Sans-Culottes*. Sounds like a wild game!

Germany invented the printing press and the earliest German cards were printed in Stuttgart from wood blocks. These cards had hunting scenes with dogs, stags, ducks and falcons as their suit signs, and all the court cards painted as ladies, and exceptionally pretty ones at that.

Surviving are a very fine fifteenth-century German wood-cut set of animals, the famous round cards of Cologne, with their five suits (hares, parrots, pinks, columbines and roses) and the magnificent cards made by Vergil Solis, the goldsmith of Nuremberg. The German national suits became hearts, bells, leaves and acorns.

Holland is famous for the Holbein 'Dance of Death' cards (fifteenth century), and various satirical sets (eighteenth century) including one depicting all the most notorious Papal scandals. Naturally these packs were proscribed by the Vatican and burned whenever found.

Cards were not made in England until the end of the fifteenth century (before that sets were brought back from France by the English soldiers) and all our early cards bear costumes of the period of Henry VII. Originally our 'knave' was a straight translation of the French *valet*, meaning a son, and only later did it come to mean a rogue. The alternative 'Jack' was originally 'Jack a naipes', naipes being the Spanish for cards.

There have been very few alterations in the basic design of English cards—at least so far as serious card players are concerned—but in 1628 the card-makers received their Royal Charter, and from then on the cards bore registered marks such as the Great Mogul, Henry VIII, Valiant Highlander and Merry Andrew. In the late nineteenth century these marks became the property of anyone

*18th Century Single Headed.
Court Cards*

who cared to use them, but were an indication of comparative quality. The Great Mogul cards were premier quality, the Merry Andrew cards the least estimable. Collectors of cards can also have fun with the duty (first imposed in 1710) which varied from 3d to 2/6d. The fanciful ace of spades, containing within its design the duty stamp, developed from the card-maker's device.

In 1832 Thomas De La Rue was granted letters patent to produce both backs and fronts of cards by letterpress and lithography, and from 1862 imagination ran riot amongst cardsters. Perry and Co. manufactured waterproof cards, De La Rue added rounded corners and indices, Bancks Bros pioneered double-headed cards (1867) and soon afterwards advertising packs made their appearance. Deeking and Co. produced sets of caricatured politicians; there is even an incomplete but charming set designed by Thackeray. The joker was an American invention of the mid-nineteenth century; the plastic card also developed transatlantically a hundred years later.

Prices depend on many variables, completeness and condition being naturally important, but the earliest De La Rue packs are particularly desirable and fetch £100 or more. Seventeenth-century handpainted English or French cards are about £25 each, eighteenth-century cards a little less. For myself I collect Monopoly sets from different cities around the world. Does anybody else?

Books: *A History of Playing Cards* by R. Tilley (Studio Vista, 1973)
    Collecting Playing Cards by Sylvia Mann (H. Baker, 1973)

Postcards

Why did I write to you? One wakes up one fine morning to find that one is a rare being surrounded by imbeciles, and groans to see so many pearls thrown to so many swine.
           Marie Bashkirtseff to Guy de Maupassant

I was browsing in the Royal Standard Antiques Market in Blackheath, wondering whether I should buy a 78 of Danny Kaye singing 'Confidentially' or splash out on 'Music, Music, Music' as well, when I spotted a very large box full of intimacies. Over a thousand postcards I should think, and the stall-holder seemed not to care for them very much. 'Oh, you can have *those*,' he said, implying that everything else he had was beyond price, 'for thirty bob.' I didn't quibble (don't, when you know you have a bargain) and trotted home with my prize.

I wanted to read the things. There were probably two hundred from Percy to Dorothy in a fine Roman hand and maybe a hundred from the coy Dorothy back to Percy. Surely the romance must have ended happily, for how otherwise could the two collections have been merged into one?

Since then I've always fancied old postcards. They are so cheap, so easy to acquire and there is so much of interest attaching to them. Once I found a photograph of Mussolini hanging from his lamp-post; another time a whole album of Gladys Coopers. Watching her beauty mature and fade was not unlike watching those natural history films with speeded up action in which the life cycle of a flower is reduced to a few seconds. The ones that haven't been written on, I write on and send to my friends. Much cheaper than the ones in the newsagents.

The picture postcard was invented by the Austrians in 1869, but our own post office, with the public interest as much at heart then as now, forbade anything pictorial until 1894, when the back of the postcard was to be given over entirely to the address, and half the front was for the message. But from 1900 the system which has been in use ever since (picture on one side, message and address on the other) was permitted. The postcards, which were mass-produced in Saxony for the entire world market, sold for a half-penny and until the end of the First World War, second class postage was just a halfpenny too.

Edwardian Bathing Belle

Humorous 1950s Card

Early postcards were used to commemorate such cheering events as the death of Verdi and the assassination of King Humbert. 'Having a good time, wish you were here' must have then been more than just the analgesic platitude it is today.

Gladstone had announced publicly that he used postcards; after which (as with Gannex raincoats) the fashion really caught on. By the First World War there were fifty million postcards in the mail each week. But when the war ended the postal charges rose abruptly and that, combined perhaps with the increasing availability of the telephone, was that.

For the collector, a tray of assorted postcards is irresistible. Some hunt for churches, or railways, or agricultural scenes, or royalty, or patriotic scenes, or war scenes, or views of High Wycombe—for others it is the post-mark which is the attraction. The work of Louis Wain (the funny cat man) and Raphael Kirchner and, of course, Donald Magill are collected. So too are pin-ups (they've recently found their way into Sotheby's) and society beauties and actresses.

The going rate for postcards of no apparent interest is 5p. I price royalty and war and actresses and humorous scenes at between 12p and 20p. And there is always a reduction for quantity. For the novelist, the social historian and the nostalgic voyeur, that is cheap at double the price.

Books: *Picture Postcards of the Golden Age* by T. and V. Holt (MacGibbon and Kee, 1971)
Picture Postcards by Marian Klamkin (David and Charles, 1974)

Potlids

Oh who needs money
When you're funny?
The great attraction everywhere
Will be Simon Smith and his amazing dancing bear.
                                        Randy Newman

What has the end of the fashion for wigs to do with Pegwell Bay shrimps? Ask a silly question and you get a silly answer, the silly answer in this case being potlids. Silly things. Not too silly perhaps when they were used to preserve and advertise whatever was in the pots. But utterly stupid now. Utterly stupid, and, for this reason, sneakily seductive.

The end of the fashion for wigs (ah!) meant that pomade (or pomatum) was to be worn on a gentleman's locks. ('Does Lord Byron's hair curl naturally?' 'Naturally every night!' was the old joke.) The same social necessity that produced the potlid also therefore produced the antimacassar. (Macassar was an unguent for the hair made by Rowland and Son and represented to contain ingredients from Macassar, a district of the Island of Celebes.) The pomade in the potlids, however, was known as Bear's Grease—although probably there was nothing bearish about it, the name sounded rough and tough and masculine—and as a consequence the early potlids were decorated with a series of sixteen designs of bears at play and at bay; these are keenly hunted down.

The four Staffordshire potteries chiefly responsible for the manufacture of potlids were Mayer Brothers and Elliot, Ridgeway of

Cauldon, Ridgeway of Shelton, and Pratt's of Fenton. When Bear's Grease lost its glamour everybody turned to fish-paste (not to put on their heads, you understand, but to put in their pots) and the 1850s fashion for Pegwell Bay shrimps (ah!) ensured the continuance of the potlid business. Jesse Austin of Pratt's developed a multi-colour printing process, enabling him to reproduce the works of famous contemporary artists as well as his own works. Charming seaside views and nautical subjects were also featured.

At the Great Exhibition (and subsequent exhibitions) potlids were much in evidence, but then in 1879 Jesse Austin died, and at about the same time everyone decided that they had eaten enough potted shrimps for the time being. The industry was mortally wounded. Crosse and Blackwell struggled on, but both of them succumbed in the end, although pots of Gentleman's Relish with the original design on the lid appear every Christmas.

A word about forgeries. Since the original copperplates may be used for colour printing transfers it's possible to produce a potlid very close to the original. But an expert can still differentiate. One test is to strike a questionable potlid with another piece of china. If it's genuinely old the potlid will sound dead; if it rings true it is reproduction—but of course you may be left with two hands full of broken china.

I hope you aren't because genuine potlids are worth a lot of money. Early bears (invariably black and white) are £45 upwards and at a big country house auction in Old Windsor I saw a potlid of the Thames with Windsor Castle in the background, framed (potlids have often been framed in circular ebony frames for convenient wall-display), sell for £100; nor are prices up to £400 unheard of. But I also saw four Victorian potlids knocked down for £11 at Harrods Auction, cheap enough even if they were reproductions.

It's objects like potlids which cause me to wonder what the collectors of 2076 A.D. will treasure. Shippam's paste pots (attractive enough) or Penguin biscuit wrappers (irresistible)? The safest thing is to keep everything!

Books: *Underglaze Colour Picture Prints on Staffordshire Pottery* by H. G. Clarke (Courier Press, 1970)
    Price Guide to Potlids by A. Ball (Antique Collector's Club, 1970)
    Collecting Potlids by Edward Fletcher (Pitman, 1975)

Sheffield Plate

Here's metal more attractive.
Hamlet by William Shakespeare

Sheffield plate was invented by Thomas Bolsover between 1740 and 1743. It was killed off brutally when Elkington's of Birmingham introduced electro-plated nickel-silver in 1840. So it had just a hundred years of existence. It was invented because it was cheaper than silver; it was killed because it was dearer than electro-plate. It was nice. In the beginning Thomas Bolsover, a Sheffield cutler, used his new process for buttons, but then Matthew Boulton adapted it in his Birmingham factory to produce anything that could be made in silver. And since Regency was a good period for silver (classical elegance and simplicity) it follows that very little that was made out of Sheffield plate was ugly or tasteless. What is it? Copper sandwiched between silver foil. How recognise it? By the soft glow of the plate, which was imparted by hammering (for the stuff could not take engraving), by the marks of 'bleeding', a vivid expression for those places where the silver foil has worn off and the copper shows through, and between 1784 and 1840, by the registration marks.

Really there are three main periods of Sheffield plate. Between 1740 and 1772 you are likely to find a variety of marks (Joseph Hancock's wares are especially desirable). Many Sheffield platers marked their wares to look as much like silver as possible, so that Parliament in 1757 passed an Act, making misleading hall-marks a felony punishable by death (though this final rigour of the law was never invoked). And in 1773, when Sheffield was granted its own assay office for silver, *any* marking of Sheffield plate was forbidden, though this edict was later (1784) relaxed to permit the maker's name and device at least to appear. Between 1773 and 1784, therefore, there are no marks on Sheffield plate, but from 1784 it may be readily identified.

How to recognise it? Not simple, because of all the faking, but look first at the foot-ring. Any gleam of copper? Is the silver foil-thin? Sometimes silver wire was added to the edges to disguise the copper content; or silver ornamentation was used (especially by the interfering Victorians) to hide the tell-tale, but to the modern eye agreeable, bleeding. You'll soon become confident at recognising the real thing when you see enough of it. Also Sheffield plate is so strong that it permits beautifully detailed fretwork, and it's cheaper—even the best of it is cheaper—than modern silver. What could be more desirable?

Although Rosemary Ratcliff, who is expert in such things, fancies that replating Sheffield plate *is* permissible, it seems to be courting disaster to submit a mechanical process (Sheffield plate) to a chemical method (electro-plating). I say, let it bleed!

You are quite likely to pick up bargains in Sheffield plate at country auctions, since it is not yet as much collected as it will be in a year or two, and the prices, which depend a good deal on condition, are not as formalised as silver. Candlesticks will cost about £40 the pair, much the same as coasters. And naturally early pieces and pieces by Hancock and large pieces will be more expensive than the prices quoted here.

Books: *Antique Sheffield Plate* by G. B. Hughes (Batsford, 1970)
History of Old Sheffield Plate by Frederick Bradbury (J. W. Northend, 1969)
Price Guide to Old Sheffield Plate by Tom Frost (Antique Collectors Club, 1970)

Silver

November 28th 1666. Reflections upon the pleasures which I at best can expect, yet none to exceed this; eating in silver plates and all things mighty rich and handsome about me.

Pepys, *Diaries*

The best thing about collecting silver is that it carries with it a built-in guarantee. If you spot the hallmark and that cheery little lion passant (well, he's not always cheery; between 1796 and 1820 he looks alarmed and bewildered as if all that talk of revolution and the rights of man had got into his whiskers) and that curious leopardy face you can be fairly certain that you have got yourself a piece of silver, tested in an assay office and not found wanting. Furthermore you should be able, on the evidence of a hallmarking, to place and date your article and establish who made it. A word of warning, however. Small items of English silver are sometimes unmarked, and sometimes the mark may have worn off. As if this were not enough, a piece of silver will always be worth at least its scrap value, which can easily be ascertained by multiplying the weight of the item, which auctioneers include in the catalogue (except in the case of weighted items like candlesticks), by the current price of silver on the bullion market. And silver can easily be reconverted into money. It doesn't crack as frequently as porcelain nor chip nor come unstuck and, if it gets dented, it can be hammered out. It's nice to look at, tactile and ductile, and it profits by use. In short, if there is one area in which the bargain hunter should have things all his own way, it is silver. And yet, paradoxically, for just these reasons, it is not something to rush blindly into, for you will find that profit margins are small, sharks are savage, and there's many a man walking down the Strand with no seat to his pants because he Went Into Silver. And in 1968 silver was the thing to be into. From being 9s 3d per ounce, which is approximately what it had been for 20 years, it suddenly shot up to more than £1 per ounce. As I write this the spot rate stands at over £3. How then can one go wrong?

Silver Wine Cup
c 1600

London
1876-1895

Birmingham
1824-1848

Edinburgh
1806-1831

Dublin
1797-1820

The first thing is to learn to read hallmarks and it's alarming how many otherwise intelligent people don't. Usually you will find four punch-marks: the makers, the assay office, the quality and the date letter. The Sovereign's head may also be found on silver between 1784 and 1890 and King George and Queen Mary commemorated their Silver Jubilee by being stamped on to silver between 1933 and 1936. There exists a splendid little paperback, *English Silver Hallmarks* edited by Judith Bannister (Foulsham), which contains everything you need to know about them. It costs 60p, and you need it.

But now we come to the more vexing question of which silver to buy and how much to pay. As a rule you will do well to worry little about the famous silversmiths; if you happen upon a piece by Paul Lamerie and don't spot the master's mark you'll never know and therefore won't blame me; in any case you are more likely to win the pools or live to see a Liberal Prime Minister, so I suggest you seek out only what you can afford and in that category:
—whatever pleases your eye
—whatever can be put to use (trophies for instance are not nearly as desirable as sauce boats)
—good late eighteenth-century and early nineteenth-century table-ware (the Georgian period was the finest period whose products are generally available to modest collectors)
—Art Nouveau pieces; these are sure to hold their value and have still not been fully exposed
—Continental, Scottish and Irish pieces, where the English equivalents are too expensive; Scottish and Irish silver par-ticularly has enormous charm
—sugar casters, and pepperettes; these always seem to fetch more than the going price for other small pieces
—anything pre-1660 (I should be so lucky!)
Similarly you may avoid:
—Victorian rococo, especially those ornate pieces produced at the time of the Great Exhibition
—silver of 1697–1739 (should you ever come across any) because this is the period of silver's identity crisis when the hallmarking system was at its most confusing
—corroded pieces; carry some Duraglit with you (but wrapped up, for heaven's sake) and test anything that's tarnished. If the tar-nish is removable, fine, if not, it's corrosion
—damaged pieces; cracks are expensive to repair
—candlesticks; if you can't remove the base, it's difficult to estimate how much is silver and how much is weighting, but if you try to find the centre of gravity by balancing the candlestick on your hand, the heavier the base the less the silver content
—freemasonry pieces, Indian and Chinese silver, cigarette boxes, cigar cases and lighters, war medals.
So far as prices go (and they go a long way) I have established

the following general guidelines, which apply to auction prices within the last two years.

1700–1800
Expect to pay about £18 per ounce; probably more for sugar casters or pepperettes.

1800–1900
George IV and William IV—about £9 per ounce; Victoria—about £5.50 per ounce; less for forks and presentation cups, more for complete canteens.

1900–1976
Usually £4 per ounce for undistinguished pieces, occasionally as little as £3 for trophies, and below scrap value for cigarette cases. Sugar casters as much as £7–£8 per ounce, and more for particularly well made pieces and Liberty patterns, etc.

Books: *Silver Collecting for Amateurs* by James Henderson, CBE (Muller, 1965)
Silver: An Illustrated Guide to Collecting Silver by Margaret Holland (Octopus Books 1973)
Collecting Antique Silver by J. Bannister (Ward Lock, 1972)

Stamps

> *He thought he saw an Albatross*
> *That fluttered around the lamp:*
> *He looked again, and found it was*
> *A penny-postage stamp.*
> *'You'd best be getting home,' he said,*
> *'The nights are very damp.'*
> 'Sylvie and Bruno' by Lewis Carroll

It was part of the ritual. Every Easter down to Brighton. If the weather was fine, down to the beach. If the weather was not, down to the beach and up off it again. In any case a visit to the pier (Palace better than West) for the penny-in-the-slot machines— 'going slottish' I called it—and particularly the Ghostly House. Put in your penny and watch different spooky things happen in every room. Wow! And then a visit to the stamp shop, darker and almost as spooky as the Ghostly House. Just a few coppers to spend, but had to come away with something. One year—*mirabile dictu!*—an unperforated Queensland with Victoria's head on it for threepence.

Couldn't wait to get it home to look it up in the catalogue. And there it was: unperforated—£55. Told my big brother Simon. He remained unimpressed. Showed him *there*, look, there it *is*, look; all he said was: 'Perforation's been cut off. Margin's too narrow.' I lost my temper, threw a tantrum (I was good at that, it sometimes worked), but Simon didn't budge. At school they wouldn't think of things like that, so I showed them. Look, there it says in the catalogue, £55, and I got it for threepence! I got good value for my threepence. But I wonder what happened to the stamp.

And now Simon is a stamp collector, or rather a philatelist, because he exhibits, and wins medals, so I asked him about bargains in stamps. He said that you're not to reckon too much to the catalogue value of your stamps; and he said this is not because dealers are crooks, although some of them are 'less than completely honest'. But he said it's to do with fashion. For instance there was a great gamble, he said, when Britain issued a stamp to commemorate winning the World Cup. In a few weeks it was worth many times its face value. But it was oversold, and now it's worth barely more than it originally cost over the counter.

Simon says that to make money out of stamps, you've got to specialise until you know more about your special subject than the dealers. He says that you're certain to lose money by just buying whatever comes along, which is exactly what most kids do; Simon thinks this is a shame.

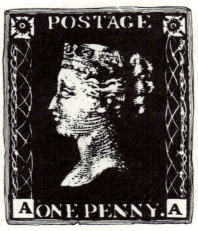

A Penny Black

You can buy from a shop. If you go to a big one like Stanley Gibbons you have a large choice and pay a large price. If you go to a smaller one you may not find what you want, but it'll be cheaper. If you buy packets in a newsagents, you're buying rubbish and paying vastly too much for it. You can buy through the post in which case if you are dissatisfied the stamp may be returned. You can join a local stamp society; your public library will put you in touch with one. These groups circulate packets into which you put your stamps for sale and from which you extract your purchases. It's fun and not over-expensive.

You can buy at auction. But you had better know your subject, especially if you patronise one of the three big houses in the UK—Stanley Gibbons, Harmer's and Robson Lowe (which is a branch of Christie's). Lots here will seldom fetch less than £10. At a smaller auction the dealers will not be much in evidence, and so the competition will be less keen. This is the ideal place to start building up a collection; indeed many of the lots will be collections.

You can buy from postal auctions, but Simon warns that these may be dealers selling their own cast-offs. In order to check, try to submit some of your own stamps, and, if you can, and if they issue 'prices realised' lists, you're in the clear. Otherwise, no dice, says Simon.

And he warns that a stamp will only be worth a tiny fraction of its catalogued price if its condition is poor. It should have all its gum, equal margins all the way round (ah! Queensland!) and not be torn or dirty. The novice who wants to see the value of his collection grow should concentrate on unused stamps in mint condition. Also he should be chary about catalogues, which are effectively dealers' buying price lists (i.e. what you'd pay if you wanted to buy). Selling prices are significantly lower. For example the current price of the current 7p stamp in the current catalogue is 5p, when it is obviously valueless. The 5p represents a labour cost on the dealer's part.

That's what Simon says.

Books: *Collecting Stamps* by Alan James (Blackwell, 1973)
The Philatelist's Companion by Bill Grunston (David & Charles, 1975)
Beginner's Guide to Stamp Collecting by Kenneth Anthony (Pelham, 1971)

Stevengraphs

And I wove the thing to a random rhyme
For the Rose is Beauty, the Gardener Time
'A Fancy from Fontenelle' by H. Austin Dobson

I am sorry to have to go back to the Edict of Nantes. I had hoped
not to have to mention the emigration of the Huguenots and the
history of how Coventry became the centre of the silk-weaving
industry. The introduction into Britain of the Jacquard Loom in
the mid-nineteenth century is not the stuff dreams are made of, but
it's necessary to know about such things if you are to understand
how Thomas Stevens became established in Coventry in 1854 as a
manufacturer of silk ribbons. Well, silk ribbons were profitable
enough, but silk-woven bookmarks were the line to be in. (With a
suitably moral text on a bookmark, the schools would snap them
up as cheap, useful and improving prizes for good scholars.)
Thomas Stevens began to search around for other outlets for his
talents. Valentine and Christmas Cards, emblematic sashes, silk
calendars, lavender sachets and hat bands, he turned his hand to
them all. And then in the early 1870s he produced his first silk-
weave pictures. They were not then called Stevengraphs, but
Textilegraphs, and they were spaced along ribbons so you could
buy them by the foot or by the yard. Alternatively you could buy
them mounted on board at a shilling a time. After 1860 you could
ask for your picture with a frame and you got a little black and
gold one with a label and a date on it, thus ensuring the delight and
fulfilment of collectors a century later. To begin with, and with his
usual canny appraisal of public taste, Stevens provided hunting and
sporting scenes, and his vigorous colours and cunning perspective
shading made horse racing an ideal subject. The backgrounds were
muted but the foregrounds vividly tinted and detailed. Amongst his
sporting series, boat racing Stevengraphs ('At The Finish') and
cricketing ones (W. G. Grace fetched £145 in 1968 and is still
scoring) are notable.

He also produced mechanical subjects, heroes (Lord Roberts for
£17, Kitchener for £19 and Parnell for £31 in 1974), religious and
legendary pictures ('Leda and the Swan' is highly desirable, having
risen from £120 in 1968 to £470 six years later), and Royal and
Commemorative subjects (the Prince of Wales fetches double
Queen Victoria, and the American Series, produced for the

164

Columbian Exposition of 1893, is as popular as American scenes always are in the British export market).

Sadly, by the end of the century the quality was deteriorating; the colours were drab and many pictures were copied directly from engravings. The twentieth-century Stevengraphs are quite undistinguished, and artistically it was only proper that the Coventry factory should be destroyed in the air raids of 1940.

In the fifties we had green girls and flying horses and ducks and Vernon Wards; in the sixties pop-art posters and the beginnings of the Beatrix Potter and Arthur Rackham revivals. But none of these, I think, display the energy of the early Stevengraphs and it's only on record sleeves, which must surely become a collector's item soon, if they are not so already, that I can see a popular art form which is really straining at the leash.

Book: *Stevengraphs and Other Victorian Pictures* by Geoffrey Godden (Barrie & Jenkins, 1971)

Teapots

Who is the Potter, pray, and who the Pot?
The Rubaiyyat of Omar Khayyam trans. Fitzgerald

Once I had a sauna beside a Finnish lake. The birch twigs had been bundled that morning by Finnish children who ran along the bank shouting slogans at us. In the sauna we became impregnated with the scent of the forest, and after plunging naked into the lake we put on woolly things and hunched around a huge cauldron full of butter and pepper and tiny fish which we had trawled from the lake. Later, as the sun failed to sink below the horizon, the Finnish housewives sang to us until tears drenched their cheeks.

It was ethnic. It was poetic. And I was reminded of it while researching into teapots. You see, originally there were no teapots. You sat ritualistically in front of a pot of boiling water in which camellia leaves were drowning. In due course you sipped the potion from tiny egg-shell glazed bowls and wisdom came to you, and knowledge of the infinite. From this to PG Tips is a squalid story.

Tea came to Britain some ten years after coffee, in the middle of the seventeenth century. And the Chinese teapot (from Yi-Hsing near Soochow) was copied by the Delft potters, and so to Bradwell Wood, Staffordshire where two Dutch brothers named Elers set up their kiln.

The early British pots were small (with tea at £1 a pound, no wonder!) and squat, but to the basic teapot structure many artists applied their skills. Among these were John Astbury and the great Thomas Whieldon, Whieldon's apprentice, Josiah Spode, and his partner, Josiah Wedgwood, the men at Leeds and Chelsea, Bow and Derby, Langton Hall, Caughley (the birthplace of Willow pattern) and Worcester, where from 1751 the firm built its reputation mainly through its teaware in the name of the enigmatic Dr Wall.

But then from Europe came neo-classicism and along with Adam, Sheraton and Hepplewhite, the teapot manufacturers turned to Greece and Rome for their ideas. Wedgwood produced its portentous Jasper-Ware (and still does) and its mournful black basalts, while Nantgarw copied early Sèvres patterns, Worcester went in for shells and feathers (the Flight and Barr dynasty); Spode specialized in cupids and coloured panels, and Castleford's in extravagance; Prattware's gaiety and the delicacy of New Hall combined to produce teapots of supreme elegance.

By the end of the eighteenth century oval shapes had replaced the earlier globular models and in the nineteenth century pots climbed up off the table on decorated stands and china feet (notably the delectable Rockingham) and became ornate and fanciful and grandiose, the size of the teapot reflecting the size of the Victorian family. Some Victorian teapots, notably one produced for the Great Exhibition, were just about as big as the Queen herself who could have comfortably curled up like a dormouse inside. Blue and white transfer-printed pieces became popular and remained so. Wil-

Enamel + Gilt Teapot
1867

Brass Teapot
1896

low pattern, Indian Tree, and Copeland's Blue Italian pattern are still as popular in the 1970s as ever they were and I can guarantee to sell them immediately from my stall, whether antique or modern.

About the turn of the century the fashion for country matters (Scholar Gypsies and Shropshire Lads and Thomas Hardy folk) popularized cottage-ware teapots in the shapes of, well, cottages and caravans and such. These are simple and witty and beginning to be collected. At about £12 each they are excellent value.

Although at a recent Isle of Wight auction a 'Flight and Barr White 10″ Oval Teapot with lid on stand, carrying scenic panels in full colour of Abergavenny Castle and a view near Limerick' fetched £90, you should still be able to pick up a handsome Victorian teapot for a fiver or so, which is, after all, little more than you would pay for a modern mass-produced one.

It seems likely that the tea bag and universal sex education will lead to the demise of the teapot, just as instant coffee will lingeringly kill the coffee pot. Will a 1970s Woolworth's teapot seem as strange to future generations as some of the curiouser teapots of the past (the one that poured two cups at once, the one that offered a choice of teas, the Doulton Patent Self-Pouring Pot) do to us? I hope not for, try as I may, I can find no aesthetic pleasure in a tea bag, however many perforations it may have, and I look back with longing to the tea drinkers of Yi-Hsing (and the Finnish sauna-bathers come to that).

Book: *Teapots and Tea* by Frank Tilley (Ceramic Book Co., 1957)

P.S. Should you be in that fine city, Norwich, I recommend a visit to the Bulwer Collection of 612 teapots at the Castle Museum.

Tins

It has long been an axiom of mine that the little things are infinitely the most important.
The Adventures of Sherlock Holmes by Conan Doyle

It was one of those revolutions that affected the lives of everyone in the country and yet it was non-political, non-sectarian, and bloodless. You wouldn't have registered that it was happening until it had happened, and then you might have regretted it, or welcomed it. I refer to the invention of tin-making machines in 1872 which revolutionized the English packaging industry. By the end of the nineteenth century manufacturers no longer packed their smaller items in wood, unless they wished to appear deliberately old fashioned; everything was tinned.

Huntley and Palmers were the storm troopers. Their biscuit tins were designed to look like inlaid mahogany, or fisherman's creels or book bindings or jewel caskets or almost anything other than biscuit tins. Chocolate tins would be blacksmiths' anvils or hearts or bells, money-boxes would look like pillar-boxes. Lozenge tins would be shaped like lozenges. Tins were issued to commemorate

coronations (and still were for the Coronation of Queen Elizabeth II) and patriotic tins warmed the hearts of our drenched troops in the First World War and occasionally deflected an enemy bullet. A great deal of ingenuity and a fascinating variety of popular art was expended upon these tins, which were painted or printed by offset lithography or transfers. I collect early gramophone needle tins. The ones with the His Master's Voice trade mark on them are so engaging that I would never offer them for sale.

Well, just recently tins have become most respectable. Andy Warhol immortalized (or immoralized) a Campbell's Soup tin and Roger Opie had an exhibition of tins at the Victoria and Albert.

Obviously they are now about to be furiously collected and I recommend that you buy up all and any that you can find post-haste. On my stall their prices range from a modest 50p to £1·50 but James A. Mackay suggests in his *Encylopedia of Small Antiques* that transfer-printed and novelty tins can fetch as much as £50, while offset lithoed tins are in the range of £15–£40; he may be right although I have to add that I have never encountered such extravagant prices, even at auction. But of one thing you may be sure; before very long I will!

I can't recommend a book on tins because I haven't seen one, but 'Tins-N-Tiques' (Fridays, 185 Westbourne Grove and Saturdays, 125 Portobello Road) specialize in such things. And the *Country Life* for 7 December 1961 (which I'm sure you'll have somewhere about the house) has an article by Alec Davis, 'History Printed on Tin'.

Toby Jugs

Ah well, it's a poor heart that never rejoices. Put the Toby this way, my dear.
>   Gabriel Vardon in Charles Dickens's *Barnaby Rudge*

Toby Jugs are weird objects, more alarming, to my mind, than charming, and not at all suggesting the 'good cheer and good company' which Lord Mackintosh of Halifax, who collected them, insisted on. To me a Toby Jug is more eloquent as an awful warning against prolonged drinking bouts, but everyone to his taste; they do have an interesting history and are much in demand.

Tobies came from the Staffordshire potteries and grew out of the cream-coloured saltglaze stoneware figures made by John Astbury and Thomas Whieldon. From these came the hollow receptacles with moulded seated figures; a handle at the back and a spout at the front of the tricorne hat to facilitate pouring. The fun begins when one speculates on why these figures became formalised into Tobies and who Toby was.

Could he have been Sir Toby Belch? Improbable, because Toby wears eighteenth-century dress and Sir Toby wore doublet and hose. What about Laurence Sterne's Uncle Toby, featured in *Tristram Shandy*? The date is about right. Ralph Wood of Burslem produced the earliest Tobies about 1770 or a little earlier, and

Toby Jug - Ordinary Model about 10" High

Tristram Shandy appeared piecemeal during the 1760s. The trouble is that Uncle Toby was an old soldier and dressed like one, and not an old soak. Could he have been Paul Parnell, a Yorkshire farmer who died in 1776 and who is said to have consumed £2,000 worth of Yorkshire stingo? Or Edward 'Toby' King, who had a coffee house at Coventry?

No, he is none of these, if one is to believe the authorities, and who else is there to believe? He was surely Harry Elwes, nicknamed Toby Fill-pot (or Phillpot) who died 'as big as a Dorchester butt' from excessive drinking. And here is what happened to him after *that*:

> 'His body, when long in the ground it had lain,
> And time into clay had resolved it again,
> A potter found out, in its covert so snug,
> And with part of fat Toby he form'd this brown jug;
> Now sacred to friendship, and mirth, and mild ale;
> So here's to the lovely sweet Nan of the Vale.

171

Thus runs a popular ballad called 'The Brown Jug'.

Ralph Wood (who was succeeded by his son of the same name) was an artist and knew his public, and his 'ordinary' models were instantly popular (much as the Doulton Tobies reintroduced in the thirties and featuring contemporary and fictional figures were). They were 10–11 inches high (though he also made miniatures), and from then on constant variations on the theme were played by any other Staffordshire potter worth his saltglaze. There were even

Martha Gunn.

Mr Micawber
Royal Doulton

Sam Weller
Royal Doulton

female Tobies, modelled after Martha Gunn, a Brighton bathing woman who used to dip the Prince of Wales, and consequently bore his feathers on her hat. (In 1918 a Martha Gunn was sold at Christie's for the then record sum of 600 guineas, which only goes to prove what a good-looking and dedicated lady can achieve at Brighton.)

You should look out for jugs marked R. WOOD, or Ra Wood,

or Ra. Wood, Burslem, with perhaps an impressed pattern number. Enoch Wood, Neal & Palmer, John Walton, Ralph Salt and Pratt are other desirable early makes of Toby Jugs. And of course the Victorians churned the things out unendingly. As to prices, late Victorian Tobies can be had for as little as £5, and I've had a chipped one on my stall for 50p—and no one's been gasping to get it at that modest price. But you'll be unlikely to find an early one for less than £50, and you could pay a great deal more. Please don't.

Book: *Collector's Guide to Staffordshire Pottery Figures* by Hugh Turner (MacGibbon & Kee, 1971)

Toys

But yesterday she played with childish things,
With toys and painted fruit.
Today she may be speeding on bright wings
Beyond the stars! We ask. The stars are mute.
'The Dead Child' by George Barlow

All the earliest manufactured toys came from Germany. But very few of these early toys have survived; and the ones which have are expensive. Bavaria and Saxony were the centres which produced working models of toy trains, as well as cheap tin toys such as penny whistles, clockwork clowns and performing monkeys.

In Britain we had model coaches and Noah's arks, farms with primitive animals and modest wooden 'Bristol' toys, which were made in cottages and small shops. Early rocking horses dating from the seventeenth century were more like boats than horses, with side pieces upon which the horses legs were painted. Other early toys included roller-skates, jack-in-the-boxes, yo-yos and bows and arrows. In the nineteenth century there were Sunday toys, including picture blocks of religious subjects and educational card-games based on the Happy Families idea.

The earliest jigsaws, dated about 1765, were mounted and boxed in mahogany and made by Wallis and Son, Mapmakers; as you might expect, they depicted maps.

For girls there were toy mangles and sewing machines, which actually worked, tin ovens which boiled a tiny saucepan of milk over a candle flame, flat irons and cleansing utensils; everything, in

Teddy Bear
1910

Pedlar Doll with wares
c1830

short, which could be found in the kitchen was made in miniature for the toy-room.

For boys there were train sets; early metal ones date from the 1870s and were so beautifully detailed by scientific instrument-makers (Bassett Lowke is the name above all others to look for here) that they're hardly toys. More recently Hornby and other firms have produced excellent scale models with charmingly varied track and rolling stock.

Other mechanical toys include clockwork horses, carriages, boats and roundabouts, crawling babies and monkeys on sticks, barrel organs and dancers. Toy banks from the USA are currently very popular: a bulldog which tosses a coin into the air and catches it in his mouth; a soldier who fires a coin at a pigeon; a footballer who kicks a coin into a goal; and, commonest of all, the 'Jolly Nigger Boy', who lifts the coin to his mouth and swallows it. Many of these cast-iron toys, which were produced between 1870 and 1910 carry the names of real American banks, but were exported to

174

Britain in large quantities. A few, notably the 'British Lion' and 'Tommy', were made here. Many are currently being imported from Taiwan with the sinister words 'Made in Taiwan' erased. 'Clown, Harlequin and Columbine' is exceptionally rare.

Toy theatres are fascinating—in this context a visit to Pollocks Toy Museum is essential—not least to those who study theatre history. The scenery and mechanics of these beautiful toys represent the Victorian theatre at its most elaborate—and decadent. Naturally they are not cheap and are seldom found in good condition.

Musical automata are scarcely toys at all, in the sense that they were to be looked at and not played with, but they have a magic

Penny Toys c 1900

which would enchant any natural child, and some of them (particularly the birds in cages, which sing as they hop from perch to perch) are triumphs of mechanical ingenuity.

Most of all these are rarely found at bargain prices, and you might be wiser to concentrate on the Penny Toys, which date from the turn of the century (although even then they cost rather more

175

Clockwork Duck with flapping wings original price 9¾d

Clockwork Woman with Mop

than a penny). These are tin models, usually German, no bigger than three and a half inches; without much detailing, they give a fair and cheerful account of bus and aeroplane, balloon and cab and fire-engine. You should not pay more than a few pounds for these. In contrast, a magnificently detailed model of a horse and cart complete with driver and load of vegetables, for which (greatly daring) I recently bid £50—the most I've ever bid for anything—at Phillips, was sold for £110. But I'm just as happy with my black and white dog, which set me back a fiver but which, when I squeeze his squeezer, yelps and wags his tail and hops across the floor.

Books: *Antique Toys and their Background* by Gwen White (Batsford, 1971)
Illustrated History of Toys by Fritzsch and Bachmann (Murray Sale, 1966)

Treen

In old times we had treen chalices and golden priests, but now we have treen priests and golden chalices.

John Jewel, 16th-century Bishop of Salisbury

Edward H. Pinto is the man. He it was who, with the obsessive single-mindedness of a pile-driver, amassed in his house (Oxhey Woods House) and garden a vast collection of some seven thousand treen objects, most of which are illustrated in his definitive *Treen and Other Wooden Bygones* (G. Bell & Sons, 1969).

You are anxious. You are confused. You are not quite sure what 'treen' is or are. Never fret. Treen is a generic word for anything made out of a tree, and, commonly, any 'miscellanea of small wooden objects in daily domestic or family use and in trades and professions'. (The definition is Pinto's.) Thus it may incorporate such things as artificial legs, back and head scratchers, dog tongs (for separating fighting dogs in church), ox muzzles, muffin prickers, tennis-ball brushes, podgers (for feeding the meat into sausage machines), beekeepers' bellows (for subduing inimical bees), mole traps, warbler discs, lark traps and bird scarers, hectorgraphs and zograscopes, tatting shuttles, niddy-noddies (or cross-reels), lace-makers' bats, wig-powdering carrots (very rare and desirable, these), glovemakers' donkeys, wimbles (for twisting straws), and clickets (or snappers) for calling inattentive pupils to order at dame schools.

Treen objects made up the stock-in-trade of apothecaries, costumiers, gourmets, and wine-bibbers, fire-lighters and fire-fighters, chefs and cooks, lavenderers (later known as launderers), letter-writers, games-players, printers, sailors, fishermen, scientists, coffee-house owners, textile workers, tobacconists, woodworkers, teachers and horologists.

In short—and about time too—anything that's useful and small and made of wood is treen. And it is collected, though those who do so have problems which other collectors do not face. It is always difficult, often impossible, to date treen. It has no hallmarks, touchmarks, design books, nor heroes. Obviously there are clues to be obtained from identifying the wood, but with over 60,000 different hardwoods and a hundred or so softwoods, this is not always easy. Radio-carbon tests will establish when the tree died from which the object was made, thus providing an *ab quo*, but how to discover your *ad quem*? The style of the article, documentary records and the purpose to which the object may have been put are other clues, but inadequate for most treen.

So you may not be able to date it, perhaps cannot even identify it, yet its vagueness is part of its charm. Mr Pinto used to keep one corner of his exhibition (now removed to the Birmingham Museum and Art Gallery) for mystery objects, and visitors would enjoy guessing the use to which these exhibits might have been put. In any case, now that you have read this chapter, you will be able to refer to your wooden egg-cup or pepper-mill, cigarette-box or potato masher as your 'treen', thus inspiring in neighbours and casual visitors a proper sense of admiration and inferiority, than which nothing is more satisfactory when you are feeling miserable or inadequate.

Prices vary hugely, of course. I think it would be misleading to cite any examples, because the variations are so extreme. But treen is not generally expensive, though good examples soon will be.

Books: Mr Pinto's (see above)
    Treen and Other Turned Woodware for Collectors by Jane Toller (David & Charles, 1975)

Valentines

> *Girl, if you was a boy and I was queer*
> *I could go for you.*
>   Norman Mailer

I was about to say that the Valentine was dead when I noticed, it being St Valentine's Day, that the whole of the back page of *The Times*, and part of an inside page as well, was devoted to Valentine messages, wistful, crude, adoring, dismissive, erotic, eccentric and shy. *The Times* had promised a volume of love poems to all its Valentine advertisers; but even the Thunderer evidently failed to recognize the enormous wealth of love, fulfilled and expectant, at large in the country, for they ran out of love poems and had to offer a single boxed rose instead. If only all that love could be exploited, like North Sea Oil, if only cars would run on it and children eat it and cattle graze off it and people shelter under it. Instead of which it's allowed to run riot; they don't even tax it; no wonder we have to borrow from the Arabs.

It all stems from the cruel martyrdom of St Valentine on 14 February, 270 A.D. He had the foresight to die on the eve of Lupercalia, the day that had always been linked with fertility, thus immortalizing himself in a myriad of bad verses. For centuries it was the custom to send presents on St Valentine's Day, but in the eighteenth century it became the thing to send a hand-written billet-doux, coloured and decorated with lovers' knots, hearts and other sentimental imagery. You could lift your verses and flattering phrases from manuals produced for just this purpose (even today some local newspaper offices have similar volumes containing suitable lines of doggerel for memorializing a relative), and you took great care over the lettering.

The first printed Valentines surfaced in 1761, flimsy things with hand-coloured engravings, some by Bartolozzi, no less, and ballads. By the turn of the century H. Dobbs and Co, fancy paper manufacturers, had begun to mass-produce Valentines, the earliest of which may be recognized b the inscription: 'Dobbs Patent'. Should you find one of these, treasure it. 'Dobbs & Co' means 1816–1838, 'H. Dobbs & Co' 1838–1846, 'Dobbs & Bailey' 1846–1851, 'Dobbs & Kidd' from 1851.

In the early years of the nineteenth century better quality paper was imported from Germany, and this permitted pierced and em-

Comic Movable Valentine

bossed borders and elaborate paper lace framing up to two inches wide. By 1825 almost half a million Valentines were being sent through the post and since, at this time, postage was computed by the number of sheets enclosed, and an envelope doubled the cost of postage, Valentines complete with their own lacy envelopes were produced; these are now scarce and zealously pursued.

At about this time 'trade' Valentines which the tradesmen sent to the domestic servants were introduced and the history of the Valentine thereafter becomes two-tier, posh and unposh. Posh people's Valentines became intricate and elegant, using etching, lithography, simulated flowers, ribbons, Gothic cut-outs, shells, gilding and feathers etc. Crimean War Valentines contrasted the rigours of war with the tranquillity of the English countryside, Cupid's Telegrams promised to pay the bearer '£ove' on life-like bank-notes, and bills demanded payment of 300 kisses. A Valentine might contain a miniature portrait, a flower spray painted on ivory, a tiny concave reducing mirror or a photo in a locket-like frame. By the 1870s over one and a half million Valentines were posted annually and one large firm calculated an annual outlay of £2000 on scent and £1000 per week on artificial flowers. The workers, however, had to make do with comical, spiteful and vulgar Valentines, and parodies of domestic bliss.

Valentine Postcard 1905

The Valentine was hard hit by the fashion, which Gladstone publicly approved, for picture postcards (q.v.), and the custom died out abruptly with the First World War. But in the year of the General Strike, Raphael Tuck celebrated their centenary year with a series of Valentine cards and everyone started loving one another again—well, almost everyone.

And there was always the cunning way in which Valentines could be used to test your spouse's faithfulness. You sent him/her two cards and waited to see if he/she would tell you about both of them!

Prices? Well, pre-1840 Valentines, complete with envelopes, can fetch anything up to £100, and lacy ones or elaborate Victorian examples will set you back £20 at least, but for the rest a few quid will do the trick. The cost, that is, of inserting an advertisement in *The Times*.

Book: *Collecting Printed Ephemera* by John Lewis (Studio Vista, 1974)

Miscellaneous

> *at the market place*
> *we sell many things*
> *including love & courage*
> *but these you must bring*
> *with you*
> *and pay for as you leave*
> William Wantling

I've always been slow. Caroline said I was when she gave me my first French kiss on the Lizard Peninsula. I thought Caroline was fast, but now I realise that she was no faster than the others. I am slow. I was still learning to rock'n'roll when the twist came in, and still learning the twist when they started doing the mashed potato. I kept *meaning* to get to Biba's, and was just about to when it went out of business. Consequently the nostalgia boom took me by surprise, and I've still not quite come to terms with things being collectable which I bought first time around.

It's Bevis Hillier's fault. His book *Austerity Binge* (Studio Vista) chronicled the history of design in the forties and fifties, and he's writing one now on the sixties and seventies. The implications are alarming. Will our popular designers become so self-conscious that they will add a 'nostalgia quotient' to all their products? What will happen when (having mortgaged our future in the North Sea) we find that we have also marketed our entire past? When London Bridge and the great Cunarders went it was the beginning of the end. What price Wilson's Gannex?

The message is clear. Throw nothing away. That Barkers carrier bag, that threepenny bus ticket, that portable record-player which plays only 45s, those Beatles T-shirts, those Snoopy money-boxes, anything in bakelite or plastic or formica or wrought iron. Early televisions with doors, sticks of rock, beer bottles—in a word *tat* is in. Keep it all. I do. I may have been slow with Caroline on the Lizard Peninsula, but I'm not going to be left out now. I've just splashed out 15p for a 'Keep Britain in Europe' badge.

Now for a quiet canter round some other collectibles which didn't merit a whole section to themselves.

Isle of Man
Fire-Brigade

Livery Button
Grocers Company
1890

Railway
Brass.

Buttons are big, so to speak, in America, where they even have a *National Button Bulletin*. The most interesting area of buttoneering is probably the amassing of livery buttons and buttons with family crests on them, but don't ignore uniform buttons (fire-brigade and railway as well as the armed services), porcelain buttons by such notable firms as Minton and Wedgwood, and French enamel buttons.

Door-porters (or Stoppers or Stops, as they are now usually called) were made from cast-iron or brass, marble or pottery, carved wood or bottle-green glass. They became necessary towards the end of the eighteenth century with the introduction of the door-hinge which closed your doors automatically, and many of the early ones came from iron-founders, keen to display their skills with flat-back iron or bronze models of celebrities. The Coalbrookdale Company and the Canon Foundry were pre-eminent, and historical figures, animals, bells, Punches and Judies and regimental door-porters

*Punch + Judy Iron
Door Porters
1849*

were all popular. After the First World War shell-cases (often engraved by the men in the trenches) were employed. Being capitalist swine we use an old company seal as a door-stop.

Gramophone records are things which I have enjoyed displaying on my stall from time to time, and have more than once made a useful profit on bankrupt stock of LPs and EPs bought at auction. But

78s are the most interesting for collectors, as a browse through *Record Mart Magazine* (40p monthly from 16 London Hill, Rayleigh, Essex) or *Vintage Record Mart* (30p from the same address) will show. And it is not the angelic Ernest Lough singing 'Oh for the wings of a dove' which fetches the big money. Nor is it Gigli nor Peter Dawson nor Bing nor Clara Butt nor Fats, not even Louis. These were produced in such quantities that they are easily obtainable. No, what the buffs are really after are early Elvis Presleys. And the Platters. And the Ink-Spots. In short it is early rock'n'roll records which are to be pampered and treasured (you can pay up to £45 for a single disc), but scarcely ever played just in case . . . A strange world. A strange obsession.

Run-of-the-mill 78s sell for 10p–15p each. But they sound far better played on a wind-up gramophone with wooden or steel needles than they do on your modern stereo monster or quadraphonic God.

Menu-cards became necessary when, even in middle-class Victorian households, meals stretched to five courses and more. The card-

Doulton Menu-
Card Holder
1886.

Tablet Form
China.
Menu Holder

holders could be made of silver, china or plate, while the cards themselves were of hand-painted cardboard or fringed silk or satin. It was thought elegant to have matching cards and doyleys. And in passing the **Doyley** was named after Thomas Doyley, the Queen Anne Warehouseman, whose doyleys were both 'cheap and genteel' and which consequently made his fortune.

Napkin-rings, which began to be used in the early eighteenth century are pleasant to collect, since they are representative and cheap examples of the work of all the great silversmiths. Naturally they would not have been used at big dinner parties, when the napkins would have been folded in elaborate shapes and patterns (my sister Janice can make water-lilies) but the following morning they would have been slipped through napkin-rings for family use. Since they were only used by upper-class families, most old napkin rings are extravagantly made, often incorporating in their designs names and monograms and crests. Besides silver, gold, silver-gilt, mother-of-pearl, ivory and wood were popular materials.

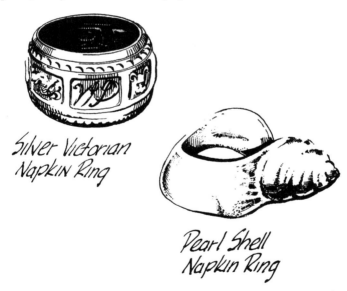

Silver Victorian
Napkin Ring

Pearl Shell
Napkin Ring

As with napkin-rings **pincushions** are ideal for collecting; readily available at accessible prices in many styles and materials, they represent a vanished world. Do people still have leisure to make beautiful yet unnecessary things? They knit and sew, but that saves

185

money and can be done in front of the television. Some pincushions are quite enchanting. I sold one for £3 (far too cheap) in Tunbridgeware. It was a perfect model of a little kettle. I wish I'd kept it. Regency pincushions and early Victorian ones were thin and flat and in fancy shapes such as swans, bellows or wheels. These could fit conveniently into reticules, but as the nineteenth century advanced and things swelled and puffed themselves up, so did pincushions. Sequin and pearl encrustations on velvet stuffed

Victorian Stuffed Pincushion

Sailor's Pincushion

Porcelain Pincushions.

with kapok; muslin, ruched and ribboned and decorated with patriotic slogans and such; where pincushions were concerned anything went: patchwork, beadwork, tortoiseshell, silver, ivory, ceramics, papier-mâché, metal—there was no end to the ingenuity expended in finding new ways to store pins. I used to keep them in the lapel of my jacket. *Sic transit gloria mundi.*

Spoons are interesting. Caddy spoons for use with tea-caddies originated in England and the large bowl allowed plenty of scope to a fanciful craftsman. Scallop-shells, acorns, jockey-caps, vine-leaves, fish, all may be found on caddy spoons. Some had points on the end of the handle to prevent tea-leaves clogging the spout of the pot. Christening spoons and crested spoons, condiment spoons

Silver Spoon c 1800

Kidney Shaped Caddy Spoon 1813

George II Silver Ladle

(you can still buy little silver salt spoons for under a pound) and ladles are all easy and rewarding to collect. I particularly like the china spoons from tureens and sauce boats which are frequently painted with country scenes on handle and bowl. These are about

£3.50. Any silver-plated flatware (the posh name for cutlery) may easily be re-plated.

Books: *Buttons for the Collector* by Primrose Peacock (David & Charles, 1972)

Buttons (A Guide for Collectors) by Gwen Squire (Muller, 1972)

Small Antiques for the Collector by D. C. Gohm (Gifford, 1969)

Small Antiques for the Collector by Therle Hughes (Lutterworth, 1964)

Collecting Gramophone Records by E. T. Bryant (Soundbooks, 1962)

In Conclusion

Why do we sneer at the man who says 'I don't know much about art but I know what I like'? That man is a hero, a survivor of the days when everyone knew what they liked. We need prompting. We have forgotten how to respond. 'We must ask children and birds how cherries and strawberries taste.' What has killed our taste buds is that we have been taught by other people about 'good taste'.

Many people have a vested interest in good taste. Advertising agents need to claim it on behalf of their clients. Retailers need to claim it on behalf of their goods. Money is involved. The pressures are great. But the great thing is that you are free to back your judgement against theirs, *and it will cost you less.*

The message of this book is to ignore everything, if necessary, contained in it but to retain this one sentence: BUY WHAT YOU LIKE AND PAY WHAT YOU CAN AFFORD.

There are so many beautiful things in the world that we become dazzled. There are so many ugly things in the world that we become blinded. But if we blink frequently and look carefully and trust the evidence of our eyes we'll be all right, we'll manage, we'll get by. Good luck.

Specialist Reading on China

Blue and White: *Blue-Printed Earthenware 1800–1850* by A. W. Coysh (David & Charles, 1972)

Bristol: *Old Bristol Potteries* by W. J. Pountney (EP Publishing, 1972)

Caughley: *Caughley and Worcester Porcelains 1775–1800* by G. A. Godden (Herbert Jenkins, 1969)

Chelsea: *Chelsea Porcelain, The Triangle and Raised Anchor Wares* by F. Severne MacKenna (F. Lewis, 1969)
Chelsea Porcelain, The Red Anchor Wares by F. Severne Mac-Kenna (F. Lewis, 1967). (A third volume by the same author and from the same publishers on the gold anchor period is out of print.)

Coalport: *Coalport and Coalbrookdale Porcelains* by G. A. Godden (Herbert Jenkins, 1970)

Davenport: *Davenport Pottery and Porcelain 1794–1887* by T. A. Lockett (David and Charles, 1972)

Delftware: *English Delftware* by F. H. Garner and Michael Archer (Faber and Faber, 1972)

Derby: *Derby Porcelain* by F. A. Barrett and A. L. Thorpe (Faber and Faber, 1971)

Doulton: *The Doulton Lambeth Wares* by Desmond Eyles (Hutchinson, 1975). (Mr Eyles' definitive and beautiful book *Royal Doulton 1815–1965* (Hutchinson, 1965) is out of print.)

Goss: *The Price Guide to the Models of W. H. Goss* by Roland Ward (Antique Collectors Club, 1975)

Lowestoft: *The Illustrated Guide to Lowestoft Porcelain* by G. A. Godden (Herbert Jenkins, 1969)

Mason's: *The Illustrated Guide to Mason's Patent Ironstone China* by G. A. Godden (Barrie and Jenkins, 1971)

Minton: *Minton Porcelain of the First Period (1793–1850)* by G. A. Godden (Herbert Jenkins, 1968)

Nantgarw: *Nantgarw Porcelain* by W. D. John (Ceramic Book Company, 1948, two supplements added 1956 and 1969)

New Hall: *New Hall and Its Imitators* by D. Holgate (Faber and Faber, 1971)

Rockingham: *The Illustrated Guide to Rockingham Porcelain* by D. G. Rice (Barrie and Jenkins, 1971)

Spode: *Spode: A History of the Family, Factory and Wares from 1733–1833* by Leonard Whiter (Barrie and Jenkins, 1970)

Staffordshire: *History of the Staffordshire Potteries* by S. Shaw (David and Charles, 1970)

Swansea: *Swansea Porcelain* by Ellis Jenkins (D. Brown, 1970)

Wedgwood: *Wedgwood* by Wolf Mankowitz (Spring Books, 1966) *The Collector's Book of Wedgwood* by Marian Klamkin (David and Charles, 1971)

Worcester: *Royal Worcester Porcelain* by H. Sandon (Barrie and Jenkins, 1973)

Further Reading

Recommended general books on antique collecting
(N.B. The list could be endless. These are just some of the books which I have found helpful in compiling my book.)

John Bedford: *Looking in Junk Shops* (Max Parrish, 1961, reprinted Macdonald)

John Bedford: *Still Looking for Junk* (Macdonald, 1969)

Collector's Encyclopaedia of Antiques (Collins, 1974)

A. W. Coysh: *The Antique Buyer's Dictionary of Names* (Pan, 1970)

Jüri Gabriel: *Victoriana* (Hamlyn, 1969)

Hampden Gordon: *The Lure of Antiques* (Murray, 1961)

Bea Howe: *Antiques from the Victorian Home* (Batsford, 1973)

Therle Hughes: *Small Antiques for the Collector* (Butterworth, 1964)

The Lyle Official Antiques Review for 1975/6 (Lyle Publications, 1976)—includes typical prices raised at auction throughout the year

James A. Mackay: *Antiques of the Future* (Studio Vista, 1970)

Patrick McVeigh: *Antiques, a Guide to Sensible Buying* (J. Donald, 1974)

John Fitzmaurice Mills: *Collecting and Looking after Antiques* (Hamlyn, 1973)—especially useful for repairs and restorations

Arthur Negus & Max Robertson: *Going for a Song* (BBC Publications, 1969)
George Savage: *A Dictionary of Antiques* (Barrie and Jenkins, 1970)
G. E. Speck and Euan Sutherland (editors): *English Antiques* (Ward Lock, 1969)
Antiques: A Pop Guide for Everyone (Octopus, 1973)

Index

192